Red Velvet Rebellion

A Spiritual Awakening Disguised as a Relationship Disaster

Minerva Morehart

First published by Morehart Books 2026

First edition

Paperback ISBN: 979-8-9943424-0-4

Author's Note

This book is a work of nonfiction, told from the author's perspective and based on her memories, reflections, and lived experiences. As with all memoir, events are filtered through personal perception, and others involved may remember them differently.

Some names and identifying details have been changed to protect privacy. In places, dialogue and minor details have been reconstructed in service of narrative clarity and emotional truth.

Dedication

For Quinn, who made everything worth it.

The truth will set you free, but first it will piss you off.

—Gloria Steinem

Contents

Introduction

In Roman mythology, Minerva is the goddess of wisdom and inner strength.

For much of my life, I wasn't operating as a Minerva.

I acted like a Minnie, the decidedly non-goddess type—the sort with beige furniture, beige emotions, a beige marriage, and boundaries so soft they barely counted.

Minnie was the part of me that believed being chosen mattered more than anything else.

I hadn't always been beige. I once had dramatic, unnaturally red hair. I danced tango at an erotic arts festival and covered my condo in pink shag rugs three inches deep—subtlety wasn't really my thing.

But slowly, as Minnie took over, I twisted myself into someone smaller and duller—not because love required it, but because I thought it did.

Minnie was trying to help. She believed in a prophecy, pushed for a vasectomy reversal, and led me into a marriage that went spectacularly wrong.

It turns out a red velvet couch—bold, sensual, and gloriously unnecessary—was exactly what I needed. The day I ordered it, I was done shrinking.

That was the day I became Minerva.

Chapter 1. The Yoni Whisperer

Portland, Oregon, Spring 2008

By thirty-eight, I'd decided I was done being divorced. Five years was plenty, thank you very much. I was going to find a nice, attractive man who was willing to ballroom dance. I would toggle my status back to "married," and I would finally be whole again. With that goal driving me, I burned through potential dates on OKCupid as if my life depended on it. Some panicked part of me believed it did. I never went more than two weeks without a date. No luck in finding "The One" yet. That only made me double down.

I was feeling pretty good about the latest guy, though. There was nothing obviously special about him on paper, but I felt pulled to him in a way I couldn't explain, especially since we'd only emailed so far. It didn't make much sense, but it was time to talk on the phone for the first time and see if it might actually lead somewhere.

"So," I began, settling into my kitchen chair to interview him for the job of future husband, "tell me about your previous relationships.

What have you learned from them that will prevent you from making the same mistakes again?"

I'd just added this question to my process after too many romantic face-plants. I had a PhD in psychology. I understood patterns. Applying them to my own life was another matter. This time, though, I hoped I'd finally cracked the code.

Ryan's OKCupid profile had been promising—attractive in a rugged way, funny, and sensitive. The icing on the cake was that when he messaged me, he'd mentioned he wanted to learn to dance. I knew he'd only said that because he had seen in my profile that it mattered to me, but at least he was willing, unlike just about everyone else.

"Well," Ryan's voice was deep and velvety on the phone, "I rushed into my previous relationships."

I waited for more. There *had* to be more.

"I choose better now," he said to fill the silence, sounding like he thought he'd answered the question completely.

I nearly choked. *Choose better?* That's it? After two divorces and other failed relationships, his grand insight was that he'd developed better taste in women?

"Right…" I said slowly, already mentally composing my polite goodbye. This was exactly the kind of non-answer that told me everything I needed to know. No self-reflection. No responsibility. Just blame.

"I appreciate your honesty," I continued, biting back my disappointment over striking out yet again. "But I think we're probably looking for different things…"

Just then, my doorbell rang.

"Oh, hey, my locksmith just arrived," I said, relieved for the interruption. "I need to go. Take care, Ryan."

"Wait, Minnie, I—"

"Good luck with everything," I said, already heading for the front door.

As I hung up, I felt that familiar mixture of disappointment and resignation. *Another one bites the dust.* At least I'd figured it out during a phone call rather than wasting an entire evening on a date.

The locksmith (handsome but shorter than me) fixed my deadbolt while I mentally moved on to the next potential match in my inbox. Ryan had seemed promising on paper, but the phone call had confirmed it—another man who blamed everyone but himself.

When I checked OKCupid again that night, Ryan's name appeared in my inbox, and I almost deleted it without reading. What could he possibly have to say that would change anything?

But curiosity won out.

Minnie,

I gave you a BS answer on that phone call… but you deserved better.

Look, I've had some pretty craptastic screw-ups in my relationships, but when I think about it, I have learned quite a bit…

He went on to admit he'd been conflict-avoidant in his first marriage, lost himself trying to please his second wife, and had a pattern of chasing emotionally unavailable women. His casual tone mixed vulnerability with his tendency to deflect serious topics with humor.

Maybe this doesn't change anything, but your question really got to me… If you want to give me another shot, I'd love to take you to that fancy-schmancy tea place you mentioned and have a face-to-face convo.

The man who'd given me a throwaway answer about "choosing better" had just written something thoughtful and unexpectedly vulnerable.

I read the message twice, then closed my eyes.

Damn it.

I decided to meet him in person.

Maybe this one would be different. At the very least, I'd get a good cup of tea.

* * *

Three days later, we met at the tea shop where Ryan would later say I was making "compulsive eye contact." It was true—I was studying him like a research subject, trying to see straight through him.

He was an interesting mix. He managed security personnel for a major corporation in Portland, and that seriousness showed when he talked about work. But he was also the guy who wrote about being "craptastic" at relationships and apologized for giving me "BS answers." All of that seemed at odds with the gentle energy he exuded in person. I wanted to know more.

A week later, he bought me a single white tulip at the Portland Saturday Market and listened with genuine curiosity as I explained the difference between a tango and a foxtrot. "So, the foxtrot is like… more smooth and flowy?" he asked as he waved his arms to show what he meant. It was adorable.

At three weeks, we had dinner at a little Ethiopian place and went dancing at the studio where I taught. Ryan was getting better, though he still counted steps under his breath with the seriousness of defusing a bomb. "I may have stolen one of your dance DVDs for some emergency cramming," he admitted sheepishly after executing a surprisingly decent box step. "Couldn't have you thinking you were dating a complete dance catastrophe." It was endearing.

To celebrate our "one-month anniversary," we had dinner at my favorite Indian restaurant and went to *Sweeney Todd* at Keller Auditorium. My ex-husband and I had held season tickets there throughout our marriage—and even after—and I'd suggested the theater without thinking. I didn't realize I was testing whether Ryan could share that part of my life: the cultured partner who'd share my love of live theater. At least for now, he seemed to be passing.

* * *

Even better, my new boyfriend gave amazing massages.

"Turn over," Ryan said. His hands were warm against my shoulders. "Let me work on your back now."

We were in my bedroom, six weeks into our relationship. I rolled onto my stomach, letting my face sink into the pillow. His hands found the tight spots under my shoulder blades, applying just the right amount of pressure. "Wow, you carry a lot of tension here," he murmured. "It's like you've got knots on top of knots."

"Occupational hazard of teaching dance. And hunching over my computer too much. And, you know, existing in the world."

I moaned involuntarily as he worked over my whole back.

I was letting my guard down in ways that surprised even me. After my divorce, I'd developed pretty solid defenses, but Ryan had this way of being completely present that made those walls feel unnecessary.

His hands moved lower, tracing the curve of my spine, then back up toward my shoulders. Suddenly, his touch changed—became lighter, more hesitant. His palms hovered just above my skin.

"Huh, that's really interesting," he said quietly.

"What?" I turned my head to look at him, but his eyes were closed in concentration.

"There's something…" He paused, his hands still suspended over the center of my back. "It's hard to explain. Like there's this energy right here." His right hand moved to hover over my heart. "Something's guarding this."

The words hit me like a gentle electric shock. I felt tears spring to my eyes before I even knew why. "I don't know what that means," I whispered, though something in me recognized the feeling.

Ryan's eyes opened, and he looked down at me with such tenderness that my chest ached. "It's okay. You don't have to know. I just… I can feel it. Like there's this beautiful, bright light inside you, but it's all wrapped up in armor."

A tear slipped down my cheek and onto the pillowcase. How could he see that? The walls I'd built so carefully I'd forgotten they were there?

"Sebastian," I said, the name coming out as barely a whisper.

Ryan's hand settled gently on my back, steady and reassuring. "Your ex-husband."

I nodded, not trusting my voice. How do you explain to someone you're dating that you've loved another man so completely that you've never figured out how to fully open your heart again, even though you want to? Even though the divorce had been mutual, some part of me was still guarding against ever loving someone so completely again.

"He didn't hurt you, did he?" Ryan's voice was protective.

"No," I managed. "The opposite. He loved me so well that when it ended… I guess I decided never to be that vulnerable again. But I want to be… I'm just afraid."

Ryan was quiet for a long moment as his hand made slow, soothing circles on my back. "That makes total sense," he finally said. "But maybe… maybe that part of you is ready to trust again. With the right person…"

I turned over to face him, studying his eyes. There was no judgment there, and no impatience. Just acceptance and something that might have been hope.

I smiled and touched his face. "I like to think so."

He leaned down and kissed me, soft and unhurried, and for the first time in years, I felt those walls lower just slightly. Maybe my search was over.

* * *

A month later, we'd settled into what felt like a real relationship, and I was very happy with how things were going. He was still learning to dance, and we had even gone to "Kissing School," a six-hour introductory tantra workshop with exercises such as tender hand-kissing, intimate eye gazing, sensual back-to-back dancing, and soothing foot-massaging.

"So, what are you thinking for this weekend?" I asked him as we cleaned up after a Thursday night dinner. "Maybe we could check out that farmers' market on Saturday, or catch a movie?"

"Oh, actually," Ryan said, loading dishes into the dishwasher without looking at me, "I'm going to be pretty busy this weekend. The guys and I are planning a new D&D campaign, and we need to get all the details worked out before we start next month."

I paused, a salad plate in hand. "The *whole* weekend?" I knew he loved his role-playing gaming nights with his friends, but come on… There was no time for me at all? I'd even be willing to do some role-playing of our own.

"Yeah, probably. You know how it is with D&D prep—we've got to build entire worlds, figure out character backstories, map out these epic story arcs… It's seriously intense stuff. Way more complicated than you'd think." He said it casually, as if it was no big deal.

"Right," I said slowly. "When did you decide this?"

"We've been trying to nail down this thing forever. You know how it is with a bunch of guys—getting everyone's schedules to align for an entire weekend is like herding cats. But we finally figured it out last Friday."

I set the plate down carefully. "And you didn't think to mention it to me before now? That you'd be unavailable all weekend?"

The casual way he'd said it—as though he were mentioning groceries—made our time together feel optional to him. After ten weeks of building something that felt serious, I was suddenly just a Thursday-night companion—pleasant enough for weeknights, not important enough for weekends.

Ryan's shoulders tensed slightly. "We don't live together. I didn't think I had to clear my weekend with you."

Ouch.

True. But still, I expected a heads up about weekend-long commitments. I think most people would.

"It's not about clearing anything with me," I said, trying to keep my voice level. "It's just… letting me know. That's all. I was looking forward to spending time with you."

"We spent time together tonight."

"Right. Thursday night dinner. How romantic."

I immediately regretted the sarcasm, but I was frustrated. Ryan sighed and turned to face me. "Look, Minnie, this isn't just some random game night. This campaign is a big deal, and these guys… we've been gaming together forever. It's kind of our thing."

"I'm not saying you can't play your game, Ryan. I'm saying it would have been nice to know about it before I spent the week thinking we might actually see each other this weekend."

He looked genuinely confused. "I didn't think it was such a big deal."

And there it was.

"It's not," I said, settling onto the couch with my book. "Go plan your dragon adventures. I'll find something else to do."

Ryan stood there for a moment, clearly wanting to say something but not knowing what. Finally, he grabbed his keys from the counter.

"I'll call you Monday," he said.

"Sure."

After the door closed behind him, I sat in the quiet of my condo and felt the shift. The man who could read my energy, who'd seen through my defenses so clearly just weeks ago, somehow couldn't see how much his casual dismissal of our weekend had hurt.

Maybe those walls around my heart weren't as unnecessary as I'd thought.

* * *

I wasn't ready to give up yet, though. He had potential. Before throwing in the towel, I wanted to give us another chance. So, I came up with a plan.

"I've been thinking," I said, picking up a piece of tofu with chopsticks, "maybe we should try more of that energy work from Kissing School."

Ryan, who had been eyeing his own tofu warily, looked interested. "Like that thing we did with feet and legs last month?"

"Yes, but more *intimate* than that. I was thinking it might help us… connect better." Things had felt off since the D&D weekend two weeks earlier, and we both felt it. He'd seemed almost lit up during the energy work from Kissing School—grounded, purposeful. It had cracked me open emotionally, and it seemed to open something in him, too. I hoped we could tap back into that.

"You mean like, working on your… uh…" He gestured vaguely toward my lap, looking slightly flustered. "Yoni?" He said the word carefully, still new in his mouth. "Would it be… sexual? Or like the other energy work?"

I hesitated. "I don't actually know exactly what it will feel like. I've read about yoni massage, but I've never had one. From what I understand, it's more like deep tissue work. People say the body stores old emotions there. It's not about getting off. It's about releasing stuck emotions."

He studied me for a moment. "So, this would be… healing?"

"That's the hope," I said. "Kissing School opened something in me—but you were the one who made it shift. When you really focused, I could feel things move. I keep wondering if there are more blockages down there, and if you might be able to help release them."

He was quiet for a moment, then nodded. "Alright. Let's give it a shot. Tomorrow."

I smiled. Things felt better between us already.

* * *

The next morning arrived with an air of possibility, but I felt unusually vulnerable. As I lit candles and turned on soft music, my body seemed to know something important was about to happen.

"Do you think this will work?" I asked. I needed him to.

"Yeah. Now relax. Let me do my thing," he said with a wink as his hands moved over my shoulders and arms.

I closed my eyes and tried to let go—of the D&D weekend, of the subtle feeling of becoming optional, of my fear that I'd have to start over again if this didn't work.

As his hands moved with intention, I softened. *This* was the Ryan I'd fallen for—steady, attentive, and unexpectedly intuitive.

I'd always imagined energy workers as wispy New Age types with beaded necklaces. Ryan looked like he belonged at the helm of a Viking ship.

And yet, he worked from some deeper knowing. Bypassing analysis. Going straight to instinct.

When his hands moved to my yoni, I focused on staying open. Each touch felt electric, as if tiny waves of energy radiated from his fingertips.

"Wow, that's really interesting," Ryan said, startling me out of my trance. "Some areas feel a little different—a little hotter or rougher. It's hard to explain…"

He trailed off as he noticed me frowning and silently resumed. I relaxed again.

I started to feel blocked energy, which I hadn't even known was there, begin to move.

Then came the emotional baggage.

Waves of old pain surfaced—without stories attached. The details no longer mattered. Only the release did.

You are safe. Let go.

And I did.

We had only been skimming the surface before, but now deeper, more painful memories were bubbling up to the surface and being released in a steady, healing stream. It felt like they simply dissolved, cleansing my yoni and my whole being of negative energy.

Ryan paused, searching my face. I could see the question in his eyes.

It was painful, both emotionally and physically, but in a good way, like a deep tissue massage that hurts at first, but then the pain releases, and it feels better. I could explain all that later, though. All I could manage in the moment was to pant, "Keep going, please," and so he did.

My body shook and spasmed as the stored emotions worked their way out—like muscles relaxing after being clenched for years.

Then—nothing. A deep sense of peace. I felt drained in the best way.

A low humming lingered deep in my pelvis—like wind moving through a doorway left slightly ajar.

I was about to ask Ryan to stop when the air shifted.

Everything went electric.

His hands hovered, motionless.

And then I felt it—a presence gathering around me. I couldn't see it, but I felt it fill me. An embrace saturated with a love so immense it was almost unbearable—too pure, too steady to belong to any human heart.

Warmth moved downward, concentrating at my center.

My awareness followed it to the quiet hum deep inside me. The doorway I had felt moments before was no longer metaphor.

Two thoughts came from the presence, clear and unmistakable:

Portal.

You will give birth when you're forty.

And I knew.

Gratitude flooded through me.

The presence lingered, then slowly faded.

I didn't have better language for it. *I was just touched by the Hand of God.*

I began to weep—in awe, in joy, in something too large to name. For Ryan. For what had just happened.

I reached for him, and he gathered me into his arms.

"Thank you," I whispered. "I'll… explain soon."

I snuggled into him, wrapped in a quiet certainty.

An emptiness I'd carried for years was already filling.

My baby was coming.

Chapter 2. A Taxing Love Story

Hysterosalpingogram! It sounded like a magic spell from *Harry Potter.*

Lying on a cold X-ray table ten years earlier, I braced myself while my then-husband, Sebastian, waited in the lobby. A nurse was about to slide a dye-filled syringe into my va-jay-jay, step one of the hysterosalpingogram, or HSG test, and I felt like I was going to be sick.

No magical creatures appeared from my mental incantation, just the nurse holding up the ominous-looking syringe, and the overwhelming smell of antiseptic.

I once saw a movie, or maybe it was a weird dream, where the main character wore a tinfoil hat to protect himself from… something. There was a maniacal doctor who would chase him with a syringe full of mysterious red liquid and try to inject it into the tinfoil-hat man. The man was terrified of the red liquid—and the syringe. I felt his pain.

God, how I hate needles. I couldn't believe I was leaning back with my feet in the stirrups, about to allow that long, silver, pointy thing to come anywhere near me—let alone *there.*

The corners of the nurse's mouth jerked upward in what was probably supposed to be a reassuring smile, but it really came across as complete boredom and indifference. At least she didn't look maniacal like the doctor in the movie—not that it helped much.

"This might be a little uncomfortable," she said. Uncomfortable is an eyelash in your eye, or sand in your shoe. As the syringe penetrated me and the dye started moving, it felt like ice creeping through my insides, freezing me forever. As panic set in, the world spun into a blur of ceiling tiles and blinding lights, and I passed out cold.

I came to on the table just after the X-ray machine finished tracking the dye as it moved from my cervix to my ovaries. The nurse was gently dabbing my forehead with a damp rag. Maybe she had some compassion after all. "It happens sometimes," she reassured me, "but the good news is your Fallopian tubes are clear."

Oh, sweet relief. Maybe my womb wasn't pregnancy-proof after all. I jumped off the table with my freshly-dyed uterus and threw my clothes back on, ready to find Sebastian and share the good news.

The nurse directed me to the doctor's office, where Sebastian was impatiently waiting.

"My tubes are clear!" I announced, still beaming with relief. I noticed the doctor frown. "That means I'm good, right?"

He scrunched his eyebrows together as he glanced at my chart again. "Yes, well, we also need to go over the results of your bloodwork."

Oh, shit. His voice didn't sound encouraging. His grim expression didn't suggest he was about to deliver positive news.

"Your estradiol levels are elevated, and your FSH—follicle-stimulating hormone—is higher than we'd like to see. Typically, when

FSH is above ten, we see a decline in ovarian reserve. Yours is eleven. That suggests your ovaries are already diminishing in function."

Sebastian's hand closed around mine; whether it was to reassure himself or me wasn't clear. "What does that mean, exactly? Are you saying she can't get pregnant?" His voice was calm, but I could hear the concern.

The doctor exhaled slightly. "Not necessarily. But her hormone levels indicate that her body is working harder than we'd expect to stimulate follicular development. That's often an indicator of lower egg quality and quantity. Her AMH—anti-Müllerian hormone—is also on the lower side, which confirms decreased ovarian reserve." He looked at me, his voice gentle but firm. "It's not impossible for you to conceive naturally, but statistically, the chances are very low. Given these results, I strongly recommend in vitro fertilization."

IVF.

The letters felt sharp. Like needles.

Just minutes earlier, I had been practically skipping down the hall in relief. Now I was learning that my blockage-free tubes might be irrelevant.

I couldn't believe it. "But I'm only twenty-eight."

The doctor nodded. "Yes, and that's why we're having this conversation now. These numbers don't mean pregnancy is off the table, but they do mean that time may be a more significant factor for you than for other women your age."

I barely heard him. How could this be happening? I had always assumed that when I was ready, it would just… happen. Mom always warned me about how easy it is to get pregnant accidentally. I'd always been so careful, until a year earlier when we had started trying. I thought that when I decided to have a baby, I'd have one. But not only had it not happened yet, now I was being told my eggs were running out like sand through an hourglass I hadn't even known had been turned over.

Sebastian was keeping it together better than I was and asked another good question. "If we decide to keep trying naturally, what would you say our realistic chances are?"

The doctor hesitated. That pause. I hated that pause. That pause meant bad things. "I can't give you an exact number," he admitted, "but with her current levels, the chances of natural conception each cycle could be in the low teens. And as time progresses, those numbers will continue to decline."

"Low teens." The phrase rang in my ears, hollow and merciless.

Sebastian looked at me with concern. "But not impossible."

"No, but it does mean that if pregnancy is a priority, I would recommend moving forward with IVF sooner rather than later."

Sebastian turned toward me, and seeing my shell-shocked expression, he gently stroked my hair. "Hey, Sweetheart," he murmured, his voice soft and reassuring. "I will always love you. No matter what. We're going to be alright, whatever happens."

* * *

After many long discussions, Sebastian and I had embraced being "dinks" (dual income, no kids). A year of trying before the fertility testing had left us discouraged and exhausted, and I didn't think I could handle the added stress of IVF—or all the needles. The expensive treatments were out of our reach, anyway. We briefly considered adoption, but we decided that wasn't for us, so we convinced ourselves we were happy and complete in our family of two.

I told myself I didn't want to be a mother—and I'd believed that lie for ten years.

It seemed strange to me now that I had given up so easily back then. What I had with Sebastian had been beautiful—quiet, intellectual, and tender. He would have supported whatever decision I made about fertility treatments, never pressuring me one way or another. That's just who he was—endlessly understanding, even when it came to giving up on our shared dream of parenthood. Even though we had tried to start a family together, our relationship felt complete without one.

Maybe deep down, I knew he wasn't meant to be the father of my child.

The spirit had said—clearly, unmistakably—that I would give birth, not adopt, so it must be possible for me to get pregnant, and my time for doing so was approaching.

Still, how could I be sure? Had I really heard a spirit, or had I just been caught in some euphoric high from the yoni massage? I wasn't someone who hallucinated, and yet… this was a lot to take in. But it had felt so real, and so certain—more real than anything I'd experienced in my waking life. I wanted—needed—to believe it.

But—*low ovarian reserves… will get worse with time…*

At thirty-eight, I wondered if my body had quietly closed a door that had once been only slightly ajar.

Even with what felt like divine guidance, I was terrified it had arrived too late.

And yet—this message, this feeling—it had to be true. I clung to it as if it were oxygen.

It was as if a light switch had been flipped on the motherhood question. My deepest desire had woken up from a long slumber. I had successfully repressed my desire for a child for ten years, but it was back—with a vengeance.

I wanted a child—and a husband—but would Ryan want that with me? He already had three kids and a vasectomy—clear signs he'd closed that chapter of his life. When we met, my dating profile said I didn't want children, and we'd never revisited the topic. If he was even willing to consider it, would he act quickly enough? Time wasn't on my side.

And if he didn't believe me about the spirit? If he thought I'd lost my mind? Well, that would end things right there, because I was on a mission now.

He might believe me, though. He had been open to the tantra workshop and the yoni massage. Why not this, too?

I didn't think it was a coincidence that the spirit had visited me while I was with him—especially in such an intimate situation. So, if I was interpreting the signs correctly, Ryan must be meant to be the father.

Maybe my search was truly over. I had been searching for my lifetime partner for years, and maybe the spirit's message was also a sign that I had found him.

I wasn't sure Ryan was my forever person, but I knew my next step: I had to find out how he felt about my sudden, desperate desire to become a mother.

* * *

The day after the spiritual encounter, we were sitting at my small kitchen table. The scent of garlic from the stir fry still lingered in the air as we quietly finished eating. Ryan cleared his throat and looked at me in expectation, with a mixture of curiosity and nervousness. I understood his curiosity, but whatever could he be nervous about? He wasn't the one grappling with whether we should have a child together—yet.

"So… did I… did I do okay?" he asked in a tentative voice. I heard all his unspoken doubts and insecurities in the pauses. "With the massage, I mean. I wasn't really sure what I was doing, but it felt like something was definitely happening. You seemed upset at one point, and I got worried I was hurting you or something."

Ah, that explained his nervousness. He must have been so worried throughout dinner, thinking he'd let me down. "The massage was incredible. I felt parts of me healing that I didn't know were there. Parts of it were uncomfortable, but then it was as if a dam burst and released all the things that needed to heal. And then it was blissful… It was amazing, and I'm so grateful you did this for me."

He looked relieved, then curious. "Partway through, you went really still. It felt like something… I don't know, shifted in the room somehow. Hard to explain. What was going on?"

Here goes nothing. "I experienced something… unusual," I began, almost afraid to admit the truth. "A… spirit… appeared and spoke to me…" I paused to see if he thought I was crazy.

Instead, he leaned closer, with an intense look of curiosity. "And…" he prompted.

"It said I would give birth when I'm forty." There, I had said it out loud. What would he do?

He looked surprised but didn't pull away, which I took as a good sign. The silence seemed to stretch out, pulling on my already frayed nerves. I suppose it had been a rather unexpected thing for me to say. "It sounds crazy, I know, but…"

"Hey, I believe you," he said softly, gently placing a fingertip on my lips. Something in me relaxed at his words. He didn't think I was crazy or hallucinating. I could tell he really believed me. He wasn't just humoring me.

"There's more I need to share." Here comes the hard part. Time to see if we would break up over this. "Well, now I want to have a baby. With you…"

He let out a small laugh. "Honestly? I hoped we would."

My entire world tilted.

"I didn't bring it up," he said. "Your profile said no kids. But if you want to try, I'll see if my vasectomy can be reversed."

I felt overwhelming relief, as if the pieces of a long-unfinished puzzle were finally coming together.

In that moment, every doubt I'd ever had about Ryan seemed to dissolve. He believed me. He wanted a child too.

My questionable fertility and his vasectomy felt insignificant in the face of what felt like destiny.

Our child—our family—felt inevitable.

* * *

Over the next few weeks, thoughts of having a baby consumed me. Laundry piled up, dishes accumulated in the sink, and non-urgent work tasks were postponed indefinitely as I fantasized about holding my little prophecy baby. Every conversation somehow circled back to fertility. Every spare moment was spent researching specialists and success stories. Luckily, I had just enough brainpower left to call the fertility clinics—or my grand plans would have died under the bed with the dust bunnies.

Ryan seemed amused by my newfound obsession, quietly stepping in to tackle the dishes or fold a load of laundry when he was at my condo, all while raising an eyebrow at the pile of mail I'd yet to open. He listened with bemused patience as I rattled off success rates and treatment options, nodding at the right times—even as his eyes glazed over.

Sometimes, I caught a flicker of something else in his expression—hesitation, maybe. Or concern about the intensity of my sudden obsession. But I didn't have time for hesitation. Urgency has a way of silencing doubt, especially when you believe it's divinely orchestrated. I would push any negative thoughts aside and launch into another explanation about vasectomy reversal methods, sperm viability, or timing. I would not entertain second thoughts. I was on a mission. He said he wanted this. That was enough.

* * *

Eventually, my research led me to the top surgeon in Portland, so I scheduled us an informational appointment. Full steam ahead.

At our appointment, after the surgeon reviewed our medical histories and fondled Ryan's balls, he was ready to make his pronouncement.

"Well, there's good news and bad news. The good news is there's a very high likelihood we can restore Ryan's fertility through surgery. The bad news," he turned ominously toward me, "is that your advanced age and previous hormonal results suggest Ryan's surgery alone won't be enough."

Seriously? Advanced age? That's so rude. I just turned thirty-nine. That's not exactly geriatric. But it was legitimate to point out my inconclusive results from years ago.

He continued, explaining that we should go straight to IVF, in addition to the vasectomy reversal surgery. Doping me up to produce more "aged eggs," painfully harvesting them, fertilizing them, and re-implanting the good ones would cost $18,000 for the first attempt, but that probably wouldn't be enough either. Subsequent attempts would be "only" $14,000, though. He didn't know how many attempts it would take, probably more than average because of my advanced age.

Ryan's vasectomy reversal would be an additional $7,000. This would be one expensive baby before it was even born. This was all entirely affordable… if we sold our cars, our kidneys, and maybe our souls.

As the surgeon kept talking, I tried to focus, but my thoughts were spiraling. I shouldn't have been surprised he thought we would need IVF, but it just didn't feel right. The mere thought of it made me feel sick to my stomach, and I didn't know if I would have the strength to handle all that. Sebastian and I had given up because I couldn't handle the stress. Why did I think it would be any different now?

But… *You will give birth when you are forty.* The spirit had said so. I had to believe the spirit was real and correct—that I hadn't just hallucinated the entire experience. This was the right time, and Ryan was the right man with whom to be pursuing this.

Ryan's voice broke into my thoughts, his hand squeezing mine gently. "Don't worry. If you don't want to do IVF, we won't."

I smiled at him, still feeling numb as the surgeon left the room so we could discuss our options in private. We eventually agreed that if the spirit was correct—and how could it not be?—then our baby was meant to be, and we wouldn't need IVF to force what was already destined. Just the vasectomy reversal would be sufficient.

"Maybe I can just sew your vas deferens back together myself," I joked, trying to cut the tension. "How hard can it be?"

"That's really not funny, Minnie."

Whatever. Where had his sense of humor gone?

But seriously, where would we get $7,000? We needed a miracle.

* * *

The very next day, our miracle arrived. Shockingly, it was from the government. As I was going through the mail at the kitchen counter, I saw an envelope from the IRS, which threw me into a mini panic attack. I wasn't expecting anything from them. What if I was being audited? Or owed money? That was the last thing I needed.

I reluctantly opened the envelope and nearly dropped it when I saw what it was—a tax refund for $7,004. I must've accidentally claimed all the pets I'd ever had as dependents, because there was no way this was right. I had only expected about $3,000 back. Apparently, I had made a rather large error in my calculations, and the refund reflected the corrected amount.

"Ryan, look at this! I know how we can pay for your surgery now."

When he saw the dollar amount, he smiled. "Well, I guess that's our answer right there. Ready to start practicing for baby-making?" He waggled his eyebrows playfully.

"Not a bad idea," I replied, while pulling him into my bedroom.

It was unbelievable. Two thoughts looped in my mind: *You will give birth when you are forty. The vasectomy reversal costs $7,000.*

What were the odds? How could that be coincidence?

It felt like confirmation. Like proof. The kind of alignment that makes doubt look foolish.

How could I question that Ryan and I were meant to have a child together, when everything seemed to be aligning so perfectly?

But whatever would I do with the extra $4?

Chapter 3. The Chalkboard of Destiny

After the tax refund provided such a strong sign that we were on the right path, two things happened:

The first was that I calmed down about getting pregnant and was able to focus on nurturing our relationship and letting it progress naturally, rather than obsessing over fertility statistics and treatment timelines. We'd only been dating four months, although it seemed like longer because of all that had happened—the spiritual encounter, the fertility consultation, and the vasectomy planning. It was a lot to pack into such a short time.

This wasn't my usual pattern. Sebastian had pursued me for nearly a year before I agreed to a first date, and even then, our relationship unfolded steadily and thoughtfully. With Ryan, everything felt accelerated—urgent because of destiny. The spirit's message had come with a deadline we needed to meet.

We decided to wait on the surgery until the timing felt right—we didn't need to schedule it immediately. Knowing we were on the right path and feeling our relationship develop was good enough for me for the moment.

The second was that moving in together felt like the obvious next step. Since Ryan had a month-to-month lease for his apartment, it was easy for him to give notice, and over the next few days—just a month after the spiritual encounter—we moved his belongings into my condo. It happened so fast that it made my head spin, but it felt right.

When Ryan moved in, some things had to change, of course. His kitchen table replaced mine. Closets were reorganized. And the pink shag rugs—the ones that had once filled every room—quietly disappeared. Beige felt more reasonable. More adult. Like the version of myself I thought I was supposed to be.

At first, everything was great. I really appreciated living with a man again. I liked the company and having him there made me feel safe and secure—something I'd missed since my divorce. I had never enjoyed coming home to an empty house. Even if I wouldn't admit it out loud, a tiny part of me always worried there might be a "bad guy" inside, just waiting there, ready to do bad things. I'd probably watched too many movies where this kind of thing happened.

Now, that irrational fear simply vanished. There was no way anything like that could happen when Ryan lived with me. Seriously, who was going to mess with me when I had my very own 6'4" security guard at home?

* * *

Two weeks after Ryan moved in, I came home from teaching pole dancing at a bachelorette party, practically buzzing with excitement. The class had been great—the women were full of playful energy, the music had been loud and invigorating, and I was in high spirits, as usual, afterwards. Such a good mood is best if shared, and I was looking forward to getting naked with Ryan.

However, he didn't greet me at the door as I'd expected.

Instead, I found him in a position I'd been seeing him in more and more since he moved in: sitting on the edge of the couch, elbows on knees, controller in hand, and eyes locked on the screen. I stood there, waiting for a courtesy pause-and-look-up. Nothing. I could've been a burglar. Or a stripper carrying beer and pizza.

"Ryan?" I called.

Crickets. Digital gunfire. No Ryan.

Well. That was… a mood-killer.

I told myself not to overreact. He didn't know what time I'd be home. *He just needs a little nudge, that's all.*

So, I put on some sultry music and began a slow striptease. Subtle? No. Effective? … Also no.

"Hey, can you turn that down a bit? I can't hear what's going on," he called, still not looking at me.

At least he acknowledged my existence. I guess.

Undeterred, I escalated the situation. Off went my shirt. Then my bra. I tossed it—artistically, I might add—onto his console.

"Whoa, careful there. You almost got me killed."

Yeah, I want your damn video game character to die. Forever.

I stood there, half-naked, watching my boyfriend give his joystick his full attention. We hadn't seen each other all day. I was trying to initiate a connection. He was trying to defeat the *Horde of Soul-Sucking Indifference* or whatever the hell that game was. I just felt so… unimportant.

I understood now why my uncle once shot his wife's sewing machine. He thought she should pay attention to him instead of spending so much time sewing. They ended up divorced, although I never heard if it was because she sewed too much or because he shot things. I used to laugh at that story. Now, I got it. Some nights—like tonight—I imagined doing the same to Ryan's console.

But a gun wouldn't solve my problem. Neither would seduction, evidently.

Part of me wanted to scream at the Horde, but another part knew it wasn't really about the game. It was just his way to unwind.

However, a very familiar feeling of rejection was stabbing my heart. For years, I had tried to make my sex life with Sebastian work. He was kind. He was gentle. He was just… secretly gay. For years, he had thought he was bisexual, but eventually, he realized he wasn't—and, as fine as my lady parts were, they were the wrong set of parts. Being rejected sexually again and again had taken a toll on my confidence. At least in the end, I had an explanation, even if I wasn't really over it.

When Sebastian and I separated, I was thirty-three and completely sex-starved. My sex drive was in overdrive, so I wanted a new man immediately—not in six months, not after healing, but *now*. I didn't want casual sex, so instead of grieving or tending to my broken heart, I threw myself into finding another relationship. I was determined to fill the husband-shaped void as quickly as possible.

I swore I would find someone who was decidedly straight and had a high sex drive. And who was also considerate and willing to ballroom dance. I thought I'd hit the jackpot with Ryan, so his rejection hurt in the most devastating way possible.

I pulled on a silky red robe to preserve what was left of my dignity and walked over to him. I massaged his scalp—something he normally loved. "Can we talk?"

"Yeah, sure. Just let me finish this level real quick." His tone was distracted and dismissive.

Still, I sat down next to him in a chair and waited, staring until he finally put the controller down with a sigh. "Okay, what's wrong?"

Oh, I don't know. Maybe the way I stripped down to my soul, and you didn't even notice…

I took a calming breath. "I feel rejected when you keep playing when I'm trying to get your attention. I feel like an NPC rather than someone important to you." I thought he'd appreciate the *non-player character* reference.

He seemed conflicted, but his expression softened slightly. "It's not that you're not important. You are. I just hate being told what to do. Both of my ex-wives constantly nagged me about the gaming, and it drove me crazy. I felt like I couldn't even unwind in my own damn house, you know?"

Both of them? Constantly?

Fantastic. This wasn't a new issue. This was a pattern—and I was walking right into it.

"I'm not asking you to stop. It's just a matter of when and how long you play. I came home wanting to connect—sexually, yes, but emotionally too. When you didn't even look up, it stung."

"Wait, you wanted sex? Why didn't you just say something?" he asked, looking genuinely confused.

Seriously? I threw my bra on the damn console, and he didn't know I wanted sex? I didn't think that had been subtle at all.

We still had a lot of figuring each other out to do. I wasn't really in the mood anymore, but when he scooped me up and carried me to the bedroom, I changed my mind.

Even so—despite the sex, despite his effort—I couldn't shake the nagging doubt in the back of my mind. Was moving in together this soon a mistake? I was starting to see the gaps between what I had thought we had—and what we *actually* had.

We were destined to have a baby together, though, weren't we? We would work this out. Surely, I was just over-reacting. I had a tendency to do that.

* * *

Over the next few weeks, things didn't improve. On a typical evening, we'd eat a quick dinner, and maybe spend five or ten minutes reviewing a new dance pattern. Then he'd vanish into his world of animated adventures for the rest of the evening.

To him, we were still spending time together—as long as I was in the room, he considered it "quality time." We weren't actually *connecting*, though. He didn't want to talk or interact while he played. Sitting in the same room while he ignored me didn't exactly fill my love bucket. I felt invisible.

It felt like, now that he had me, he no longer needed to *see* me. I knew that was an exaggeration—he did still pay some attention to me, just not nearly as much as I wanted. I'd thought living together would *increase* our quality time, not decrease it. Before he moved in, we had three to five hours of full-on connection during his visits. Afterward, we were lucky to get one.

Back when I was married to Sebastian, I didn't know about *The Five Love Languages*. He and I lucked out by having the same primary language—quality time. We spent nearly all our free time together, and why wouldn't we? We were in love.

Sebastian never made me feel like I was competing for his attention. When we were together, I was his focus. He'd set aside whatever he was doing when I walked into the room, not because I demanded it, but because that's just who he was. Whether we were cooking dinner, dancing, watching movies, or just sitting on the couch, we were paying attention to each other, filling each other's love buckets in ways I didn't even realize at the time.

Physical touch was our secondary language—also effortless. We held hands, snuggled, shared little hugs throughout the day. Even with not much sex, we were satisfying each other's need for quality time and physical affection enough to sustain our marriage for ten years—until we finally admitted that the absence of a fulfilling sex life was no longer something either of us could live with.

After Sebastian, I gradually realized that wanting to spend lots of quality time together wasn't universal. What was the point of being in a relationship if you weren't actually going to *be* together? But some people are perfectly content with parallel play—sharing space without really sharing themselves. I wasn't one of those people.

Ryan's primary love language was acts of service—the kind where he did things *for* me, not *with* me. He'd often make dinner or do the dishes (which I appreciated) but then disappear into his game for hours (which canceled out all the good feelings). He was showing love the way he understood it, but I needed presence—someone actually there with me—not just assistance.

It's not that he didn't care. I knew he did. But long stretches of quality time weren't what he needed. I tried to feel his love when he did things for me, but I'm just not wired that way.

The more disconnected I felt, the more I pulled away. The more I withdrew, the more he retreated into his games. We were both protecting ourselves instead of protecting us.

But Ryan's biggest sin—though I didn't see it at the time—was that he wasn't a straight version of Sebastian. I was comparing him to an impossible standard: a man who'd loved me perfectly, at least in the ways I chose to remember. It wasn't fair to either of us. No one should have to compete with an idealized ghost—just as no one should have to compete with pixelated zombies.

* * *

"So, where's Ryan?" my sister asked. "I thought you were bringing him. I've been dying to meet this guy who's got my big sister moving so fast."

I'd been dreading the question. Four weeks into living together, I'd expected we'd be doing more things as a couple—especially something as important as meeting my newest family members. I had told her he was coming to meet her newborn twins—because that's what he'd told me. I forced a smile, hoping my anger didn't leak through. "Oh, you know, he's busy with work. Couldn't make it." I hoped she wouldn't realize I was lying.

"Well, that's too bad. I was really looking forward to meeting him. You know, it's kind of a big deal when someone moves in with my sister after, what was it, three months?"

In truth, Ryan was at home, glued to a damn video game. When I'd told him it was time to go, he'd said his raid would take another hour. I'd said he should turn it off so we could leave. That's when he'd become all defensive and accused me of treating him like a child, just like his ex-wives used to. Well, if you act like one…

I hated lying to my sister, but I wasn't about to dissect my relationship over a bassinet. What you focus on grows. I wasn't willing to name the cracks, let alone explain that I was competing with a glowing screen every night.

My sister interrupted my dark thoughts and gently handed me a bundle of blankets with a baby in there somewhere. "Okay, Auntie duties start now. Here, support her head like this."

I pushed the blanket aside and looked down at my tiny niece. The twins were preemies, so they were both so small—half the size of my cat, so about five pounds. She had soft, pink skin and the tiniest fingers curled into fists. I suddenly understood "baby soft" at a whole new level.

Oh, how I yearned to hold my own baby. It was just a matter of time.

"God, I still can't believe there are two of them. The logistics alone are insane—double everything. Diapers, formula, childcare costs when I go back to work…"

In my heart, I was starting to question whether Ryan and I were meant to be together. There were signs pointing to yes, but I had never imagined being with someone who ignored me so much.

Even so, the clock was ticking, and part of me worried that if I let him go, I wouldn't find someone else in time.

* * *

A month later, I was tired from a long day, but I was waiting up for Ryan to return from his men's group. I was hoping for a quickie before bed, so I was reading on the couch to force myself to stay awake.

When Ryan walked in, he had the air of a kicked dog around him, but I couldn't think how his men's group could possibly have made him feel like that. This group always seemed to bring out the best in him. He went to this group the first Wednesday of every month and typically emerged with a sense of purpose and enthusiasm, not this gloom.

I reached up, placing my hand on his face, turning it toward me, but he didn't meet my eyes. Whatever was wrong, it had to be really serious.

He mumbled something about "no sex" and "thirty days," but that made no sense. "Huh?" I asked because I couldn't have heard correctly.

He still wouldn't meet my eyes. "We can't have sex for thirty days," he repeated, looking extremely embarrassed.

What? It would be like the bad part of living with Sebastian again. Completely unacceptable.

My mind raced, and I noticed my arms had crossed themselves, defensively. Weird.

What would convince him to propose a month of no sex? It wasn't as if we were old, married Catholics giving it up for Lent.

He shifted uncomfortably under my stare.

"Well, see, last month we all had to commit to some change we wanted to make and pick a penalty if we screwed up. I said I'd play video games no more than an hour a day…"

I glared at him. I couldn't believe what he was telling me. And why hadn't he told me about this the month before, when I could have supported his commitment? I would have been delighted to keep him entertained in other ways.

"I, uh, didn't stick to it, and my penalty is thirty days with no sex—starting now," he admitted in a voice one would use when fessing up about a crime, which seemed appropriate. *Thirty freaking days.* Ryan finally met my gaze, his eyes filled with regret. "I thought it would keep me on track. I didn't think I'd eff it up."

I just stared at him, incredulous. No sex for thirty days? Maybe someday, many decades in the future, I wouldn't have cared, but right now I cared, a lot.

I'd noticed he'd been cutting back on the gaming, but I'd naively thought he was doing it because it mattered to me, that he was starting to take my feelings into account. Now I knew it was because of his commitment to his men's group. It wasn't about me at all, which just added to my disappointment.

Even worse, *he* had chosen that penalty—they didn't choose it for him. Unbelievable. What the hell had he been thinking?

"Yet, here we are," I said bitterly. Then I had a thought. "Wait! Does this include just intercourse or all sexual activity?" Actually, it wouldn't be so bad if he could still go down on me. Maybe this wasn't so bad after all. It would make sense just to punish him by excluding his favorite part, but not to punish me so much.

He dashed my fledgling hope in the next instant with a simple, "All."

Un-fucking-believable.

I took a few slow breaths while I considered how to respond. He just waited.

"And if we do have sex," I finally said, "you'll have no integrity left, and that's even worse."

His face fell, and his shoulders slumped even more, as if my words made him even more miserable. Good. He *should* feel miserable. "I'm really sorry, Minnie. I didn't think this would happen. I just… I really thought I could stick to it."

Sorry didn't cut it. He was failing, big time.

"Just… go away. I'm going to read for a while." I couldn't stand being around him anymore. I wondered if we were doomed, whether I should just kick him out and fire up my dating profile again.

As he disappeared behind the bedroom door, I settled back on the couch and stared blankly at the page. This wasn't about thirty days of celibacy. It was about being a team. About making choices that included each other. About whether he understood that. What kind of husband and father would he be if this was how he acted?

* * *

During the thirty days, Ryan had no problem following through on the no-sex penalty from the men's group, even though he wasn't happy about it.

But giving up video games? God forbid he ever be asked to make a real sacrifice. He played more than ever—sometimes until 2 or 3 AM—perhaps because it was how he dealt with stress, or maybe because he'd given up trying entirely. I feared I was getting a glimpse of what our future could hold if we stayed together, and I didn't like it one bit.

The month without sex was affecting him too, both physically and emotionally. The silence between us wasn't just in the bedroom anymore—it had seeped into everything. I saw it in the way he moved around me, as if he was afraid I would shatter at any moment. We were acting like polite roommates who happened to share a bed, nothing more.

He seemed to sense something more than our sex life was off, that we were both hurting and pulling away, but he didn't seem to know what to do about it either. We clearly weren't right for each other if we couldn't even talk about this effectively.

By the end of that lonely month, I realized Ryan and I were not going to work out. The spiritual encounter while with him, the tax refund, all those signs I'd interpreted as destiny—maybe they were just coincidences after all. I had wanted to believe he could be the partner I needed, and the father of my baby, but he kept letting me down.

I must have projected too much onto him. Tried too hard to force something that simply wasn't working.

I'd thought he had such great potential, but it was being destroyed by video games and poor communication, and there was nothing I could do about that.

And then there was his history. The affairs. Maybe it was just youthful stupidity that he had outgrown. He'd admitted it to me, which suggested some maturity. But why risk it? I didn't want to become a single mom because he couldn't keep it in his pants if the situation arose.

I obviously needed to break up with him so I could search for a new partner right away. I *definitely* didn't want to visit a sperm bank. Being a single mom was a nightmare of an idea to me. My mom had filled my head with horror stories when I was young in a well-meaning attempt to convince me not to become a pregnant high school dropout, and the aversion to single motherhood under any circumstances had stuck.

I also clearly got the message that children should be born in wedlock. It was just the proper way to do things, and I still believed it would be in everyone's best interest. The baby would need his or her father and a stable home life, and I wanted a romantic partner with whom I could share a life. I wanted a family of my own, one with a husband and a child.

So, I needed to dump Ryan, find somebody new, fall in love, get married, and get pregnant—all within a little over a year so I could have a baby by forty. What choice did I have? The spirit had given me a deadline, and time was running out.

By now, even Ryan must have known we were past the point of no return.

* * *

That evening, I was standing in the kitchen sipping a glass of water, waiting for Ryan to get home from work so I could dump him. Suddenly, a little chalkboard hanging on the wall fell to the floor with a startling clatter. I jumped back and smacked my hip into the table, nearly dropping my glass.

I took slow, deep breaths until I calmed down. I picked up the chalkboard and looked at it. It wasn't blank like it had been for months—I was certain it had been empty yesterday when I'd walked past it. Now, it was covered in sweet little messages in Ryan's handwriting, written in white chalk: "I love you," "Thinking of you," and "You are my sunshine." The messages seemed to have appeared out of nowhere. Like a miracle. Where did he even get chalk? There wasn't any lying around that I knew about.

A sense of warmth flooded through me from the loving messages, but it was mixed with a sharp pang of guilt. I wasn't innocent in our declining connection—I'd been pulling back to protect myself, and that was just making it worse. How many times had Ryan tried to connect with me while I was building walls? How many small gestures had I missed because I was so focused on what wasn't working?

I didn't know when he wrote the messages, but the timing of my attention being drawn to them was uncanny. This didn't feel like a coincidence. I couldn't help but see it as another sign. It had fallen at the moment I was on the verge of walking away.

How many signs did I need? The spirit coming to me when I was with Ryan was pretty clear, but the Chalkboard of Destiny, as I now recognized it to be, suggested that, at the very least, I needed to give him another chance.

Maybe I was just looking for an excuse to not walk away, to not face another round of dating and searching. But this was too perfectly timed to be just a coincidence. I chose to believe it was another sign. Believing was easier than leaving.

And then Ryan walked through the door, as if the universe had perfectly timed his entrance, affirming what I already knew: we weren't done yet. So, instead of breaking up with him, I suggested we go out to dinner. I felt like celebrating, even if he didn't realize it.

I still wasn't sure how we were going to fix everything—or even if we could. But at the time, the message felt clear—*Ryan would be the father, so keep trying.*

Chapter 4. I Do, Take Two

One morning six weeks later, as Ryan and I were lying in bed, sweaty and satisfied, he turned to me with an unusual intensity. Things had been going really well since I gave him another chance. He'd been playing video games less, and we were connecting like we had before he'd moved in. I was happy with him and ready to move our relationship forward—and it seemed he felt the same.

He reached out and gently tucked a stray strand of my long, auburn hair behind my ear, staring at me with deep love and tenderness. I could feel it in my body—he was about to ask, and I tingled in warm anticipation.

He took a deep breath, and for an awful moment, I feared he might change his mind. But then he smiled. "I had kind of an epiphany last night. I finally get how much my gaming bothers you. So, here's what I'm thinking—from now on, I'll only play when you're already busy with something else. You'll never have to find stuff to do just because I'm gaming."

Woah. What?

That was absolutely not what I'd thought he was going to say. I mean, I was glad he'd finally realized what his gaming was doing to me and was committing to a reasonable plan. It's just that I'd thought he was about to ask me to marry him. I thought we were on the same page, but I suddenly realized we'd never talked about marriage during our previous discussions about having a child together. To me, it was obvious we should get married before I get pregnant.

However, I focused on his gaming suggestion for the moment. "Yes, that's a good plan," I said, trying to keep an encouraging smile on my face. I was glad he was proposing a workable solution to an ongoing issue. It just wasn't the proposal I expected right now.

I was still reeling from the unexpected conversation when he surprised me again.

"Marry me."

Oh, so this is a marriage proposal, after all. I had been hoping for a proposal, and here it was—but… it just didn't feel like one. Technically, it was more of a command than a question. Trying to put a good spin on it, I supposed it was kind of sexy. Maybe.

He was looking at me, waiting for a response to his command.

For a moment, I hesitated. The emotional whiplash was slowing me down. Maybe he'd brought up the video game issue first to reassure me about our future, to show he was committed to making our relationship work.

As for the marriage proposal, yes, I wanted to get married so we could get on with starting a family, but I was really disappointed with this lame proposal. So lame that, even though I wanted to get married, I felt like saying no. Sweaty sheets. Video games. No ring. This was not a proposal story I'd happily tell my friends.

Ryan was looking worried—I had delayed my response too long. The unromantic nature of the proposal didn't really matter, I decided.

What mattered was momentum, that we were on the same path, taking the next step together. The important thing was that we would get married first, then have a baby. So, I smiled and simply said, "Yes."

He immediately relaxed. "I'm sorry it wasn't very romantic. I'm just… I'm ready to commit. I didn't want to wait."

"It's fine. How you asked doesn't matter." What I really wanted to say was "Try again," but I didn't want to push my luck. I realized I would have to be clearer about my expectations with him. We didn't have the same intuitive understanding that I'd shared with Sebastian, but that didn't make our commitment any less real. Ryan just didn't see the world the same way I did and didn't intuitively understand what would make me happy the way Sebastian had. But Ryan had other positive qualities that Sebastian didn't have—like being straight.

I knew many people would question our decision, especially without knowing the full story of my spiritual encounter. They would think we were rushing into marriage, unaware of the spirit's message that drove my urgency. I didn't want anyone's opinion anywhere near this, though. What we were doing made sense to me, and that was enough.

I knew the odds were against us, both for conceiving and for making our marriage work, but I couldn't bear to believe the spirit would tease me with an impossible dream. No—we were going to get married, have a baby, and live happily ever after, despite the odds.

* * *

I knew I had to tell Sebastian. I hadn't seen him very much in the last year, but he deserved to know I was getting married again, and it was important that he hear it from me directly.

When we'd separated five years earlier, we'd signed the dissolution paperwork, but Sebastian had asked me not to submit it right away, saying it felt like "too much change too fast." So, I'd held onto it.

We remained best friends for several years, talking about everything with each other—everything except two unspoken taboos: our former relationship and any new romantic relationships with other people.

Apparently, Sebastian had found some comfort in us still being technically married after we'd separated, as did I. About a year after we'd separated, as we were walking from dinner to the theater, a monthly occurrence for us, a homeless man stopped us to ask for money, calling me Sebastian's beautiful wife. A wistful look crossed Sebastian's face, and he quietly replied, "Yes, she is," as he handed the man a few bucks. Even then, I wasn't sure how to interpret that moment. Did he want us to get back together? Was he leaning back toward being bi? If so, he never said it, and I didn't ask. I couldn't. I'd replayed that moment countless times, though, analyzing every inflection in his voice, wondering if I'd missed some signal that he wanted to try again.

For years, I'd kept hoping he would go back to being bi. Even while I was dating non-stop, a part of me secretly wished Sebastian and I could somehow reconcile. But after four years of separation, I finally had to face reality. He was never going to change his orientation, so we were never going to get back together.

I wanted more than the endless cycle of dating. I was ready to settle down again and find a life partner, not just another short-term relationship. The kind of man I was looking for—someone serious, committed, and ready for a future together—would not want a woman who was still technically married, even if she hadn't lived with her husband in years.

So, about a year earlier, I had decided it was time to legally end things with Sebastian. We weren't as close by then, which somehow made it even harder—we'd lost the easy intimacy that might have made this conversation possible. The taboo was still firmly in place, so when the moment came, I couldn't bring myself to start the conversation.

Instead, I sent him a text saying that I wanted to talk about "us" the next time we met. But when we met, neither of us mentioned it. I couldn't, and he possibly forgot or didn't want to.

Unable to break through our self-imposed silence about our relationship, I submitted the paperwork without telling him. Then I did something even worse—I went alone to finalize it, something Oregon allows when there are no disagreements or children. I wish it hadn't been allowed. I turned the end of our marriage into a cowardly, administrative act instead of the meaningful closure we both deserved.

Because I was so appalled by what I'd done, I followed up with yet more disgraceful behavior. Instead of telling him we were no longer married, I slipped our dissolution decree under his front door in the middle of the night.

Now, a year later, I was still drowning in guilt about it. I didn't want to compound that shame by marrying someone else without telling him first.

Despite our unspoken agreement never to discuss relationships, he had to hear this from me. I owed him that much courtesy. I wanted to leave as little hurt in my wake as possible and spare him the pain of finding out from someone else. So, I braced myself for our next dinner together, looking forward to seeing him, but dreading the conversation we needed to have.

* * *

As I sat across from Sebastian at the new Asian-fusion restaurant he'd suggested, I watched him charm the server, his blue eyes sparkling, his easy laugh making her giggle and blush. Strangers—men and women alike—would respond to him like that; he was just so good-looking and friendly. No one could resist him when he turned on the charm. I chuckled at his antics and sipped my wine, steeling myself for what I knew I had to tell him.

When he turned back to me, his voice softened as he asked, "So, Sweetheart, what's new with you?" I took a breath, gripped the stem of my glass, and forced the words out.

"I'm… getting married."

His fork slipped from his hand, clattering against the plate. Shock and hurt flashed across his face. "Married?" he echoed. "But we're still…" He stopped as the awful truth hit him.

I watched the realization wash over him, and my cheeks burned with shame. How had I let it come to this? A hollow ache settled in my stomach as I watched him absorb the news, guilt weighing me down.

Somehow, I managed to speak, my voice barely an audible whisper. "Sebastian… we haven't been married for about a year. I… I left the decree under your door." I paused, realizing just how awful it sounded. "I thought you knew." It sounded awful because it was—unbelievably cowardly and disrespectful.

He was silent for a moment, but then, with that gentle understanding that was so infuriatingly characteristic of him, he said, "I remember finding an envelope on the floor. I didn't realize it was anything important. I didn't open it right away, and I guess it got misplaced. I'd forgotten about it until now."

Could this get any worse? God, I want to crawl under the table and die.

I wished the dissolution hadn't been so easy, that I legally couldn't have done this to him.

Surprisingly, he reached across the table and took my hand. "Hey, it's alright," he said softly. "I just want you to be happy, and if getting remarried would give you that, then I'm glad for you." His gracious acceptance was almost too much to bear.

After a slight pause, he then told me something unexpected. "I have news too. I just received a job offer in Chicago. I wasn't sure about accepting it. I didn't know if I should move so far away. Somehow, it hadn't felt right to leave you behind, even after everything. But now—maybe it's time for a fresh start. For both of us. This job offer… maybe it's the universe telling us it's time."

Only Sebastian would weigh a cross-country move with my feelings in mind, as though he still held some quiet responsibility for me.

He really was *The Nearly Perfect Husband.* If only he wasn't gay—I'd have begged him to come back a thousand times over.

I nodded, unable to speak, as the realization settled that he'd soon be halfway across the country. Knowing he'd be so far away added a finality that hurt. I knew he was right, though. We needed the distance, this chance to truly move on.

Outside the restaurant, as we said goodbye, Sebastian reached out and brushed away my tears, his touch as tender as always, then pulled me into a hug. I melted into him and let myself savor his warmth, his familiar scent, knowing it would be the last time.

As I watched him walk away, a hollow ache filled my heart. But I steadied myself, took a deep breath, and forced my thoughts to return to Ryan. This was the path I'd chosen, the future I was determined to embrace, even if it came with a large dose of bittersweetness.

* * *

In the days that followed, I felt a lingering ache from my goodbye with Sebastian. As much as I tried to deny it, I missed him, and I feared I always would.

Still, it was time to focus on the future. The spirit's promise of motherhood was a path with Ryan, not Sebastian. I convinced myself that as long as I kept any lingering feelings for Sebastian locked away in some dark corner of my heart, they wouldn't cause any trouble.

I didn't realize at the time how deeply unfair it was to Ryan. How could any relationship survive when one person was constantly measuring the present against an idealized past?

My method of moving on was to throw myself into wedding planning and be disciplined about what I allowed myself to feel.

It seemed like such a reasonable plan at the time.

* * *

Six short weeks later, Ryan and I moved into dance position as our wedding guests clapped expectantly. They all knew I taught dance lessons part-time and were hoping for a show.

I glanced up at my new husband. In his tuxedo, with his full beard and broad shoulders, he looked like a sexy lumberjack who'd stumbled into a black-tie event. The thought made me chuckle.

"You ready for this?" he asked, and I could hear just a hint of nervousness underneath his confidence, but I wasn't worried. We'd prepared for this moment.

I squeezed his hand. "We've got this."

The opening notes of our waltz filled the room, and we began to dance. For a moment, I felt exactly as I had hoped to feel on my wedding day—present, buoyant, alive.

And as I'd predicted—he nailed it.

We moved together as one, spinning across the floor in a way that looked effortless from the outside. My red dress flared beautifully as we turned.

"You're amazing," I whispered—not only because he was dancing so well, but because he'd put in the effort. He'd wanted to get this right for me, and I really appreciated it.

"Well, I had a pretty awesome teacher," he murmured against my ear as the music ended. He winked before dipping me, and the room erupted into cheers.

I smiled for the crowd. I smiled for the photos. And I looked up at Ryan—this man I had almost walked away from more than once—and told myself, again, that I'd made the right choice.

That the way he held me now—with intention, with heart—was how he'd hold me through the storms ahead. That the man who moved with me tonight would keep moving with me, no matter where the rhythm led.

Right?

I chose to believe it.

* * *

In the weeks that followed, the distraction of planning a wedding in eight weeks was gone, and without that frantic momentum to carry me forward, the reality of truly losing Sebastian resurfaced and overwhelmed me. The finality of it—his move to Chicago, my new marriage, and the permanently closed door between us—hit me like a delayed earthquake.

I'd never properly grieved the end of our relationship, choosing instead to stay in perpetual motion. For five years, I'd kept myself too busy to feel the enormity of the loss. Now that I was married again, the whirlwind had stopped.

The grief grew until it turned into a raw, gut-wrenching, can't-get-out-of-bed pain that lived in my chest. When I'd married Sebastian, I'd given him my all. Now I didn't know how to retrieve the parts of me that remained with him. How could I ever be whole again when he still held pieces of my heart?

I wasn't even sure if I fully wanted to let him go. I felt the longing for the life we'd shared together shaking me to my core.

I knew my future was not with Sebastian, but had I made a mistake marrying Ryan so quickly? Was I really destined to have a baby with him, or had I misinterpreted the spirit's message entirely? I'd been running full steam ahead, convincing myself he was my destiny and that divine guidance would carry us through. But now, with the past pulling at me so strongly, I found myself questioning whether I'd married him for love—or just because I was running out of time.

* * *

The day it really came to a head, I was, luckily, alone in the condo while Ryan was away on a business trip. I sat on the edge of our shared bed, staring at the new ring on my finger. It didn't look or feel like *mine.* It felt like an unwanted consolation prize.

The new ring suddenly felt unbearable—like shackles. I tore it off and let it drop to the floor. What had I done? Did I have a new ring simply because I couldn't bear the absence of the old ones?

As much as I tried to let go, I was still in love with the fantasy of what might have been, if only Sebastian could have changed that one unchangeable part of himself. It was delusional to think he ever could. I knew that.

Even so, I couldn't stop thinking about my original rings. *Those* rings felt like belonging and togetherness. Unable to hold back any longer, I opened the closet and retrieved the precious little velvet box hidden in the back.

My fingers trembled as I slipped on the rings from Sebastian, feeling the regret, shame, guilt, and longing come rushing back. Wearing them felt like coming home after being gone for far too long.

As I looked back and forth between the original rings on my finger and the new one on the floor, tears slid down my neck and soaked my shirt. I pressed the rings to my chest and sobbed until my ribs hurt.

Knowing the meaning of the rings was gone forever was gut-wrenching. I knew now why I hadn't allowed myself to feel this before—it was too terrible. But now that it had started, my pent-up sorrow began gushing out. I couldn't have stopped it if I'd tried.

Eventually, the tears slowed, leaving me drained and hollow. I was exhausted, but the overwhelming feelings had passed, leaving only numbness behind. I sat there for a long time, feeling nothing.

Finally, I chided myself—it was time to grow up, to act like an adult and move on. I'd married Ryan. I'd chosen this path, and whatever feelings I still held for Sebastian would have to be buried again, like the rings I now tucked back into their hiding place in the closet.

I retrieved Ryan's ring from the floor and slipped it on, feeling its weight against my skin. I told myself I would learn to love this ring. Over time, I would associate new meaning with it.

This was my life now, and I needed to embrace it. My remaining feelings for Sebastian would have to be suppressed until they died. I needed to focus on building a future with Ryan—not on a past that could never be revived.

With my mind made up and feeling a new sense of resolve, I reached for my phone and pulled up the surgeon's number in my contacts. Ryan's vasectomy reversal was the next step in our life together, a necessary step to fulfill the spirit's promise. Even if I was conflicted about my new marriage, having a baby together was our destiny.

That was a future I could happily grasp with both hands. Taking one more slow, deep breath to steady myself, I dialed the number to make an appointment, setting the wheels in motion for the future I was determined to embrace.

Chapter 5. The Mucus Miracle

A month later, I was driving a very grumpy Ryan home from his vasectomy reversal surgery. I asked how he was feeling, even though the answer was obvious.

He grimaced. "Like someone just stabbed my balls with a knife repeatedly."

I couldn't help it—I burst out laughing. That earned me a scowl, but at least it broke the tension.

"We should've taken pictures for the baby book," I joked.

Ryan shot me an exasperated look. "Pictures of what, exactly? My junk all swollen and bruised?"

I laughed again. "I can just see our future child flipping through the album, horrified by your 'before' pictures."

He let out a reluctant chuckle. "That's really twisted."

Then he reached over and squeezed my hand. "Thanks for taking care of me," he said quietly.

I smiled—I'd achieved my goal of lifting his mood, even for a moment.

Right now, he could barely think beyond the pain. He had refused pain medication—worried about addiction—so video gaming would be his distraction as soon as we got home. We had agreed he could play non-stop all weekend while he recovered. I hoped he'd take breaks to sleep and eat, but I would leave that to him.

He'd kept his promise from three months earlier and was only playing when I was busy. Gaming had stopped being a sore spot. It was something he fit around our relationship, not the other way around, so I could be on board with this temporary deviation.

* * *

In the weeks following his vasectomy reversal surgery, I was grateful to Ryan for undergoing it, but I was annoyed with the surgeon.

At our initial consultation, he had assured us the procedure had a ninety percent chance of success. Ryan's vasectomy had been nine years earlier—below the ten-year mark when the "patency rate," the likelihood of restoring sperm to the ejaculate, typically drops. That rosy ninety percent statistic convinced us that using my tax refund for the surgery was a smart investment in our future.

As we had been leaving the clinic after Ryan's surgery, the surgeon had casually revealed the bait-and-switch we had just fallen for. Apparently, because of factors like scarring, blockages in the tubes, or sluggish sperm, Ryan's actual chances of impregnating a "highly fertile" woman—which the surgeon had reminded me, yet again, I was not—were more like forty to fifty percent. That was something I would like to have known *before* Ryan was stitched up and limping toward the parking lot.

Would we have made the same decision if we'd known the real odds? Probably—we were desperate, and time wasn't on our side. But we deserved to make that choice with full information.

In a few weeks, the semen analysis would at least reveal whether his plumbing was working again. Until then, all we could do was wait and try not to think about what we'd do if Ryan's surgery had failed entirely.

* * *

Finally, sitting in the waiting room for his follow-up appointment, I kept glancing over at Ryan, who looked oddly relaxed as he scrolled through his phone. In contrast, I could hardly sit still. I couldn't have focused my eyes on my phone if I'd tried, so instead, I sat there having a mild panic attack.

If this hadn't worked, if Ryan wasn't fertile again, I would have to question everything. The spirit's message had felt like a promise—it had been the evidence that he and I were meant to be.

Ryan glanced over at me and shook his head. "You're going to drive yourself crazy. Relax—it's swimmers or no swimmers. Nothing we can do now."

That was easy for him to say. He was already a father. It was different for me—my only chance at motherhood was riding on this.

I wouldn't relax until I knew for sure whether the surgery had worked. Had we just thrown away $7,000? Had I misunderstood the spirit telling me I would give birth when I was forty? Was I wrong about the message being real? No, it *had* to be true, so the surgery had to have been successful.

After what felt like an eternity—but was probably five minutes—Ryan was led to a small, private room and was handed a plastic collection cup.

Just before Ryan pulled the door closed, he winked at me. "Hey, do you want a picture of this for the baby book, too?"

I snorted in amusement. "Our kiddo would be scarred for life, seeing that in the baby album." I appreciated his humor, though. It helped me relax a bit.

After he was done, we waited forever again, this time for the doctor to bring us the results.

When the doctor finally walked in while reading the file, his expression was unreadable. I held my breath while he read on and on. There couldn't be that much in the report, could there? As Ryan said, it all boiled down to one simple thing—either there were swimmers or not.

"Well," he finally began, "it appears that the postoperative semen analysis indicates a presence of viable spermatozoa, suggesting functional reanastomosis of the vas deferens. The motility index is within an acceptable range for in vivo conception, with progressive motility in approximately sixty-five percent of the observed sample, indicating functional patency of the surgical site."

What? Why couldn't doctors just speak English? I looked at Ryan, hoping he'd understood something I'd missed.

Ryan looked confused for a moment too, then he grinned. "So… I have swimmers. No more shooting blanks?"

The doctor looked at him a bit condescendingly. "Well, yes, that is one way to put it."

Yes, in fact, that is a *better* way to put it. An *understandable* way to put it.

Then the success of the surgery hit me, and I was flooded with sweet relief.

It was officially *go-time* for baby-making.

* * *

My initial excitement didn't survive long. After six months of not conceiving, concern set in.

At Ryan's follow-up appointment, the doctor had reminded us that because of my "geriatric age" of thirty-nine and prior fertility history, our chances of natural conception were very low—probably near zero. IVF, he'd said, would almost certainly be required.

Despite his warning, Ryan and I had decided that if the spirit was right, then his surgery would be enough. IVF wouldn't be necessary. But now doubt crept in. What if we'd misunderstood the message? What if more medical intervention was still needed?

My fortieth birthday had come and gone over a month earlier. With each passing month, the window felt like it was closing faster.

I was tracking my fertility symptoms obsessively—charting my basal-body temperature every morning, analyzing my cervical mucus like a scientist, and scheduling our naked time with precision. Ryan, for his part, seemed to be tracking my moods instead. Maybe that was his way of helping—knowing when to encourage me and when to disappear. If so, I couldn't blame him.

We were trying for a baby at exactly the right time each month, multiple times, turning what should have been intimate moments into a checklist.

Ovulating. Check.

Sperm provided. Check.

Emotional intimacy? Deferred.

I could see it wearing on both of us.

At this point, we needed a miracle—the same kind of divine intervention that had started this whole journey—because my faith in the spirit's promise was starting to waver for the first time.

* * *

I didn't tell anyone I was trying to get pregnant because I didn't want the stress of being asked how it was going, so my friend Dora surprised me one day when she brought the topic up. She was a Native American shaman and had an unusual way of seeing things, so I guessed that explained how she knew.

I was sitting on her couch, politely attempting to enjoy a mug of stinging nettle and stevia tea. I smelled like sage because she'd smudged me when I arrived. It wasn't personal—she smudged everyone who came into her home. I used to think "clearing negative energy" was a bunch of bunk, but these days I wasn't so sure.

She was giving me an odd look, maybe seeing me clearly now that my negative energy was smudged away. "Are you trying to get pregnant?" Her question was so out of the blue, but Dora does seem to have a way of just knowing things.

"Ah, yes, actually. For six months now, and I'm getting kind of worried about it. How did you know?"

"Mmm," Dora said, tilting her head as if listening to something I couldn't hear, "you need guaifenesin. It's practically written across your forehead."

At my confused expression, she continued. "It's the main ingredient in Robitussin cough syrup, and it loosens up mucus in the nasal passages. It can also loosen up cervical mucus, making it easier for the sperm to reach the egg."

How odd. I thought it was going to be some traditional Native American herb or something.

"Your spirit baby is showing me this will open the path. It's ready to come through, but the physical pathway needs clearing first. Sometimes the spirits work through the most ordinary things—even modern cough syrup."

Well, that sounds…. hard to believe.

I had never heard of cough syrup helping conception, but who was I to go against another spiritual message, if that's what this really was.

So, even though I was skeptical of using cough syrup to boost my fertility, I told her I would try it. After all, I'd already followed other spiritual messages that led to me marrying Ryan. At this point, I was willing to risk a runny nose for even the faintest opening.

* * *

To support my decision to take cough syrup, Ryan picked some up for me, calling it my "magical mucus potion."

But for days, despite how badly I wanted to get pregnant, I couldn't force myself to take any. The ingredient list was all unpronounceable dyes, preservatives, and God knows what else.

Why is all that shit in there? Aren't some of those ingredients banned in other countries for being toxic?

I didn't want that chemical cocktail in my body, especially not when I was trying to create the perfect environment for a baby. I'm one of those health nut types who avoids artificial sweeteners, food dyes, and chemicals I can't pronounce—pretty much every single ingredient in the cough syrup—like the plague.

Although I was disgusted by the ingredient list, I stored it in my purse like a talisman, just in case desperation finally won out over my principles. I really hoped it wouldn't come to that.

* * *

A few days later, while waiting for my dance students to arrive, I felt the signs of a cold starting very suddenly. One minute I was fine, the next I had watery eyes and a stuffy nose—the works. It came out of nowhere, and it was bad.

I didn't want to be all stuffed up while teaching, so with barely a thought—and very uncharacteristically for someone who agonizes over taking a single Advil—I took a big swig of the Robitussin from my purse.

Nothing happened.

In fact, my symptoms got *worse*, and my students would be arriving any minute. I needed it to start working right away, so I took another big, thoughtless swig, hoping that would help.

Big mistake.

Almost immediately, the room started to spin like a carnival ride, and I gripped the edge of the reception desk for support. My vision blurred, and when I tried to take a step, my legs felt like jelly. *Whoa.* How was I supposed to demonstrate dance moves when I couldn't even stand up? *What am I going to do?*

Just then, my phone beeped. My students had texted an apology about being stuck in terrible traffic, so they needed to reschedule for another day. *Well, isn't that convenient?* Now I didn't have to teach while doped up. Had they texted five minutes sooner, I wouldn't have taken any at all.

I called Ryan to come and get me. There was no way I could drive like that.

While I waited for him, sitting very still, trying to keep the world from spinning, I wondered if this whole sequence was more spiritual assistance. The sudden stuffy nose, the impulsive decision to take medicine I'd been avoiding for days, my students canceling—either the universe was helping, or I'd finally snapped. Hard to say which.

When Ryan arrived and saw my glassy-eyed state, he just shook his head and helped me to the car. "Hope your magical mucus potion works," he chuckled.

* * *

Over the next few days, I was excited beyond belief because—*holy moly*—was I suddenly overflowing with cervical mucus. The difference from my accidental overdose was dramatic—I went from practically nothing to suddenly producing copious long, stretchy strands of the stuff, exactly the kind fertility books say you're supposed to have when ovulating. Apparently, this "fertile" mucus not only protects sperm from the vagina's "hostile acidic environment," but also forms microscopic highways to guide them.

Well, with the amount I was producing now, it was practically an eight-lane highway up to Uterusville.

Ryan just shook his head at me in amusement every time I shared these new bits of information. I appreciated that he didn't run for the hills when listening to my detailed cervical mucus reports.

I felt genuinely hopeful again. Maybe this was exactly what we needed to make the magic happen.

* * *

A few nights later, moments after Ryan delivered the latest batch of sperm, I felt a burst of energy deep in my womb. I went completely still. It was unlike anything I'd ever experienced.

Oh my God—that was conception.

My mind started racing between wonder and doubt. Could I have really just felt conception happening? Was it even physically possible to sense a microscopic sperm entering an equally microscopic egg? Or had I felt something even more mystical—my baby's spirit entering its first cell? Did that happen at the moment of conception, or was I completely losing my mind? The very possibility gave me shivers.

I lay there listening to Ryan's breathing gradually shift into the deep rhythm of sleep, his arm still draped across my waist. I didn't say anything to him—I couldn't. How do you tell someone you think you just felt your baby's soul arrive? Despite all we'd been through with spirits and signs, the idea still sounded impossible to me.

Instead, I held the sensation close, cradling it like the most fragile secret. As Ryan slept peacefully beside me, completely unaware that our world might have just changed forever, I stared up at the ceiling, my hand instinctively moving to rest on my belly.

* * *

Feeling really hopeful that I was knocked up, I started paying extra-close attention to possible signs of pregnancy. Every morning I checked in with my body as if I was conducting a scientific experiment.

Did I have any nausea? No.

Did I have any weird cravings? No.

Were my boobs sore? No.

Why not? *I want symptoms!*

Symptoms would have been a sign—a very welcome sign. As much as I didn't want to be uncomfortable, those symptoms would be proof there was a tiny life growing inside.

The waiting was driving me absolutely crazy.

* * *

Three-and-a-half weeks after I possibly felt the miracle of conception taking place inside my body, I was perched on the edge of the toilet, staring at the indicator window of the home pregnancy test I'd just peed on. My heart pounded as I watched the control line appear. So far, so good.

The bathroom was quiet except for the clock ticking away—the clock that was reminding me of my biological one, too. I tapped my foot against the cold tile floor as the seconds dragged on.

Conveniently, my sister had given me ten home pregnancy tests left over from her infertility saga. I'd meant to pass them along to a friend two years ago, but somehow that had never happened. Over the last few days, I'd been working my way through them, each test feeling like a tiny rollercoaster ride of hope and fear.

The first two had been negative—a control line, but no positive line. My heart had sunk both times, but I'd convinced myself it was too soon to test. Then the next several had a faint second line, almost imperceptible, teasing me with possibility. Each subsequent test had seemed to show the line darkening, but still—not definitive.

Now, this one. The sixth test. The control line popped up as expected, and then, faint at first, the second line appeared. The line didn't stop there. My breath caught. It deepened, growing darker and bolder until it was unmistakably positive.

"Oh my God," I whispered. My hands trembled as I held the stick closer. Could it really be? Hope bubbled in my heart.

The swimmers had swum. My guaifenesin-enhanced mucus had worked its magic.

I was pregnant. The test said so. It had to be true.

Except…

Maybe not.

The joy caught in my throat, tangled with doubt. What if the test was wrong? What if I got all excited, only for my period to start the next day? My chest tightened at the thought. I couldn't bear that kind of heartbreak.

In case that one had malfunctioned, I grabbed another stick and peed on it.

I looked up and saw Ryan leaning against the door frame. I had no idea how long he had been standing there. One pee stick or two? His hair was tousled, having just woken up, and he was watching me with a lopsided grin as I anxiously awaited the results.

I had purposefully not woken him up. He had believed the results of the last test, which was *clearly* inconclusive, so the additional testing was for my benefit, not his.

"So, that's what now—three, four positives in a row?" His tone was light and teasing, and his eyes were full of affection. "Are we finally going to believe it, or are you planning to pee on the entire batch before you're convinced?"

I shot him a half-hearted glare, biting back a smile. "Maybe I will. Maybe I'll pee on one every day until my period starts or a baby pops out."

He threw back his head and laughed. I chuckled at my own ridiculousness, but I still wanted more definitive proof.

The seventh test was just like the sixth: the control line, and then the positive line, faint at first, but deepening to the same unmistakable positive result.

Part of me was relieved and dancing in joy, but a small part of me still clung to doubt, whispering that it could all be a cruel trick. Two false positives weren't likely, but they weren't impossible either.

What if I was barren, after all? A year of trying with Sebastian, and six months now with Ryan. It was excruciating to be putting myself through this again, but this time, I had reason to believe it would work. The spirit would not have teased me about this.

"I'll admit," Ryan said, his voice breaking through my thoughts, "it's kind of fun to watch, but I think it's time to call the midwife, don't you? Or are you planning to build a shrine out of test sticks?"

I laughed despite myself, the sound releasing some of the tension that had been building in my chest for days. He was right—I was a little unhinged, but I couldn't help myself.

Nodding, I put the unused tests in the bathroom closet. "Yes, you're right. I'll call when their office opens." After all, I could call back and cancel the appointment if my period started.

But for now, I would let myself believe I was probably pregnant.

* * *

While waiting for my appointment in the weeks that followed, I was mostly convinced we had beaten our low odds of success, but I needed actual medical confirmation before I'd let myself fully embrace my maybe-pregnancy.

Ryan was now saying he could tell I was pregnant. "I'm telling you, they're definitely bigger," he'd say while caressing my breasts. "I'm practically a boob scientist. Very dedicated to observational research."

"You're delusional," I'd tell him, but I couldn't help smiling back.

They seemed exactly the same to me, although it's true he spent more time looking at them than I did. Maybe he was right, but I would trust a midwife more than his ogling.

* * *

My appointment finally arrived, and we spent an eternity on non-essential, time-wasting chit-chat about things like when I had last ovulated. *Come on, either I'm pregnant or I'm not. Let's get on with it.*

Finally, we got to the moment I'd been waiting for. The midwife held up a small, hand-held device. "This is a Doppler ultrasound," she explained. "It uses sound waves to detect the baby's heartbeat."

If there's a heartbeat to detect, that is. Please let there be one.

She squirted a dollop of cool gel onto my still-flat belly and began to move the Doppler slowly across my skin, searching for the baby that may or may not be in there. The room was so quiet I could hear my own heart pounding.

And… nothing.

I knew it! The home tests had all been wrong. They were expired, malfunctioning, and giving me false hope. I stared at the ceiling, blinking back tears as the silence stretched on.

But then, suddenly, a rapid, rhythmic whooshing filled the room. The sound of a tiny, steady heartbeat from our kumquat-sized baby.

I immediately burst out crying in relief. Ryan reached for my hand, squeezing it tightly. His voice was thick with emotion. "Holy shit, that's our baby." He glanced at the midwife. "Sorry. I mean, wow, that's our baby."

I let out a shaky laugh and smiled at him with gratitude and affection. The steady, strong heartbeat meant I was really, truly pregnant.

Against the odds, my baby was growing inside me. I was finally going to become a mother.

Chapter 6. A Womb with a View

I loved being pregnant, and tracking the growth of the miracle baby inside me became my favorite hobby. An obsession, perhaps. Every morning, before Ryan stirred, I'd open MidwiferyToday.com and Mothering.com like they were sacred texts. By lunch I'd read the same week's update twice, as if it might suddenly include a footnote about *my* baby.

Week by week, I'd discover what miraculous transformations were happening inside my body—even though I couldn't see or feel them yet. My baby had grown from a tiny poppy seed to a sweet pea, then a blueberry, then a raspberry, and now sat comfortably at fig-size. The weekly fruit comparisons delighted me—next week would be a lime, then a lemon. I'd actually go to the grocery store and hold the corresponding fruit, marveling at the size.

The baby's little limbs were already starting to move and stretch—though I couldn't feel it yet. Tiny fingernails were forming, facial features were sharpening, and organs were continuing to develop.

I'd memorize the latest developments and eagerly share the fruit-of-the-week updates with Ryan over breakfast. "Today our baby is the size of a fig and has taste buds!" I'd announce. He'd listen with patient amusement to my enthusiastic reports, occasionally asking practical questions like how much bigger figs were than kumquats, just to show he was paying attention.

I'd talk to my belly throughout the day, narrating my activities to my invisible companion. "Okay, Baby, we're going to teach the foxtrot now," or "Time for us to run a statistical analysis." It felt completely natural, this constant conversation with the tiny miracle inside me.

* * *

When my precious passenger was lime-sized, he had an unusual experience for a fetus: he attended a ladies-only pole dancing party.

I set up my travel pole in Dora's living room for her going-away party, right in the center of a sprawling rug. I wasn't sure if the rug would be a problem, but I figured it would be fine. Just in case, I had her friends (and my 18-year-old stepdaughter) stand around the edges.

The lesson went well. Their individual performances went well. Then came my turn…

And it did not go well.

I couldn't resist showing off a few advanced moves—big mistake. As I threw my weight around the pole to get more speed, the rug shifted, dislodging the pole. Down I went, landing hard on my very embarrassed butt.

The pole crashed after me, catching Beth's knee on its way down.

A silence fell over the room, punctuated only by Beth's sharp cry of pain. We all stared in shock as her knee swelled up and turned an impressive shade of purple.

"Oh my God, we need to call 911!" My stepdaughter Sarah shot up from her spot on the floor, already reaching for her phone. "Look at her knee—it's huge!"

"Wait," Dora said calmly, not even looking up. "Let me work with this first."

My heart raced—equal parts from the fall and the sheer guilt flooding through me. I shouldn't have been doing advanced spins. I was *pregnant*, for God's sake.

And why hadn't I checked the pole before my performance? I *always* do that. Why had I set it up on the rug? I *never* do that—it's not safe. It was all my fault Beth had been injured. Would she be okay?

Oh my God, is my baby okay? He was still so little—lime-sized, with plenty of cushioning all around him. He should be okay. *Please be okay.*

Before I could freak myself out into a full panic attack—and before Sarah could dial 911—Dora knelt next to me and pressed her hands gently against my belly. Her gaze turned distant, as if she was listening to something the rest of us couldn't hear. Her hands felt almost like they were buzzing.

"Your little one is startled but unharmed. I can feel his energy. It's strong and steady," she said with such certainty that I found myself believing her.

Before I could even thank her—or ask her how she did it—she was already moving over to Beth.

Instead of fetching an ice pack—like any normal person—Dora placed her hands just above Beth's good knee, then the injured one. Back and forth she went, humming softly.

"It's the Song of the Healthy Knee," she explained. "I'm sending it into the injured one."

We all exchanged glances. The *Song of the Healthy Knee*? WTF?

Sarah threw up her hands in frustration. "This is completely nuts," she said, shaking her head as she stormed out.

Beth, to her credit, didn't pull away. No one stopped Dora. No one *ever* stopped Dora.

Time blurred, the only sounds were Dora's soft humming and Beth's shallow, careful breathing. Five minutes? An hour? I had no idea.

I was paying more attention to Dora than to Beth's knee, so I didn't notice anything changing, but somehow, when Dora stopped humming, Beth's knee was *no longer swollen*. The bruise seemed to have vanished. It was just… gone.

Beth bent and straightened her leg, testing it. She stood, shifting her weight onto it, then looked up, stunned.

"It's fine." She gave it another cautious bend. "It doesn't hurt at all."

Beth looked around at all of us, her voice barely a whisper. "I don't understand what just happened, but… thank you."

Sarah appeared in the doorway, having cooled off, and stared at Beth's perfectly normal knee. Her mouth fell open.

"How…?" she whispered.

I wondered the same thing. First, Dora had determined *from my baby* that he was unharmed.

Now she had just performed what I assumed was a shamanic healing. I didn't have any other the language for what I'd seen.

I'd already believed in energy work from the things Ryan and I had done. But this?

This was next-level.

I stood there trying to process what I'd just witnessed. This wasn't just energy work or intuition—this was something that defied everything I thought I knew about what was possible.

Then I realized something. If Dora could communicate with my baby's spirit so effortlessly… maybe I could, too.

Carrying this tiny life inside me was already an odds-breaking miracle. But what if I could communicate with my baby before his birth? I got chills just thinking about the possibility. Now that I knew such a connection was possible, I was determined to learn how.

As we cleaned up later, Sarah admitted quietly, "I… I don't even know what to say. I've never seen anything like that in my life." The amazement in her voice matched what I was feeling.

* * *

The image of Dora's hands hovering over Beth's knee, and the certainty in her voice when she assessed my baby, stayed with me long after we'd all said our goodbyes. After her going-away party, I wanted to connect with my baby's spirit, but I didn't know how, so I tried everything.

I meditated for what felt like hours, but was probably ten minutes. (*Boring—I couldn't focus on anything but my to-do list.*)

I lit candles and sat in lotus position like some sort of spiritual cliché. (*Pointless—it just made the room smell like vanilla.*)

I hummed lullabies and random melodies, hoping the vibration would somehow carry my thoughts to the little soul inside me. (*All I got was a sore throat.*)

I tried talking to the baby with my hands over my belly. (*I only felt my heartbeat.*)

Then, one night, inspiration struck. Sebastian had taught me how to use tarot cards to find answers, which is exactly what I was looking for. I shuffled my cards, asking my baby what I should know.

Here we go. What does my baby have to say?

I flipped over the top card—and my stomach dropped.

A heart pierced by three swords.

The familiar artwork hit me like a punch. I could practically hear Sebastian's low, mellow voice explaining this exact card as we'd gone through the entire deck years ago during cozy Sunday afternoons, his tone patient as he guided me through each card's meaning. "The Three of Swords is sometimes called the divorce card," he'd said, "but remember, Sweetheart, it isn't just about heartbreak. It's about the kind of pain that cracks you open so something better can grow. Sometimes we have to break apart to become who we're meant to be."

I stared at the card, and my hands started to tremble. Was this supposed to be some kind of warning from my baby?

Sebastian's voice echoed in my mind, as clear as if he were sitting beside me: "Tarot doesn't predict the future. It reveals what you already know but haven't admitted to yourself yet. You think about your question while shuffling, then interpret the card based on your question."

But I hadn't been thinking about my marriage. Had I? And I couldn't "already know" such a thing about my future. So, this wasn't a warning from my baby's spirit. It absolutely could not be.

Could it?

No. My baby was *not* sending a warning. Ryan and I were fine. *We had to be fine.*

So, I declared tarot cards were *not* the way to connect with a baby's spirit. I shoved the card back into the deck and put them away. *That card means nothing. My marriage is fine. We're having a baby together. We're building a life. I will* NOT *be a single mom. I just didn't shuffle long enough, so the wrong card came up. Spirit babies probably communicate through dreams, not tarot cards. The mere idea is ridiculous.*

I decided the day had never happened.

However, I still wanted to connect with my baby, so I kept searching.

* * *

When my growing baby was the size of a mango, I found Kassandra.

She specialized in connecting with your Higher Self. That wasn't exactly what I'd had in mind, but it felt close enough. I hoped I would connect with my Higher Self, which would connect with my baby's Higher Self, and transmit that experience to me.

When I told her my intention, she nodded with a kind of reverent understanding that immediately put me at ease. "What a beautiful intention. The connection between mother and baby is one of the most sacred bonds. Let's create space for that communication to flow."

Kassandra's soft and ethereal voice led me into the meditation, helping me quiet the mental noise. "Just breathe into that space," Kassandra's voice floated through my awareness, "and allow whatever wants to emerge to come forward naturally."

As I dropped deeper into stillness, I became aware of something gentle pulsing around me. My aura. I had felt it before as a subtle field of energy around me, but this time I sensed a massive doughnut-shaped current extending about six feet in all directions. No wonder it feels like someone is "in your space" when they come closer than that.

As I was basking in this vibrant flow of energy, something shifted. I noticed a different flow, a second current within my own field.

It was my baby's aura.

The shock was so intense I felt myself starting to surface from the meditation. I forced myself to breathe deeply to settle back down. I focused on the sensation of two energy fields flowing together, overlapping, and connecting.

Then I realized—here was my chance. This was the moment I'd been searching for. I asked for a message, an understanding about how to be the mother this being needed, and when I tuned in, I heard it—not with my ears, but with some deeper part of myself. It was like a song—a sweet, pure song that seemed to emanate from the core of that small energy field within mine.

For a while, I just let myself feel it, afraid to move or think too hard, afraid I might lose this precious connection.

Then it seemed like some kind of maternal wisdom was pouring directly into my body. My skin tingled all over as though every cell was absorbing it. I didn't consciously understand the message, but I felt it settle deep into me, becoming part of me.

Kassandra could tell I was deep in my experience and waited for me to finish. When she sensed I was ready, she slowly brought me back to full consciousness.

When I finally opened my eyes, she was looking at me with quiet curiosity, as if she could tell something momentous had happened, but couldn't tell what.

I described what I had experienced—the torus of energy, the two fields nested together, the song, and the transmission of wisdom.

She looked startled at that. "That's extraordinary," she said, her voice hushed with reverence. "What you've described sounds like a direct soul-to-soul communication."

Her words only deepened my sense of awe. I couldn't explain it logically, but I didn't need to.

I walked out of that session feeling deeply connected to my baby. And now I knew—the connection with my baby was always there, and everything I needed to know to mother this child was already within me.

I didn't need to search anymore.

* * *

From then on, when I placed my hands on my belly and tuned in to my baby, I didn't just feel my heartbeat anymore. I felt something deeper—my baby's essence, like an internal hug that radiated warmth through my entire torso. I would get that familiar tingly feeling that spread from my belly outward, the same sensation I'd learned to recognize when connecting with spirit guides. I didn't receive clear messages my conscious mind could interpret; instead, I experienced bodily sensations that didn't feel like mine—a flutter of contentment, a wave of restlessness, or sometimes what felt like gentle amusement, as if my baby found my worrying endearing.

I also sent messages to my baby, hoping he would understand. "Head down, hands on belly," became my daily mantra—I would visualize my baby positioned perfectly for birth, with his head down in the birth canal and his little hands pressed protectively against his belly, keeping them safely away from the umbilical cord during delivery.

I was completely committed to my water birth at the birthing center—it felt right for both me and my baby. But that meant everything had to go perfectly. Any complication that deviated from textbook normal labor would mean an emergency transfer to the hospital, complete with all the medical interventions I was hoping to avoid.

* * *

One night, about a month before my due date, I had a dream I was in labor. There were tons of people in the room—doctors, nurses, student doctors—and they kept talking and talking and just *wouldn't shut up*. The constant chatter made my whole body tense, and I couldn't relax and let go. There was no way the baby was going to come out if they kept talking so much.

I was getting more and more upset, while my whole body was fighting against itself.

Finally, I snapped and yelled at the top of my lungs, "Shut the fuck up!"

Ryan bolted upright, instantly alert, his body coiled like he was ready to fight off whatever had woken him. "What's happening?" He turned to me, shoulders tense, brow crunched down in confusion as he scanned the dark room for threats.

"Sorry, it was me. Just a dream. I was in labor. It was too loud."

The tension melted from his shoulders as understanding dawned, and then he chuckled. I couldn't help but join him.

"Well," he said, still chuckling as he settled back against his pillow, "I guess we know what kind of birth experience you're hoping for."

"Yes, quiet," I said, still laughing. "Very, very quiet."

He looked at me so tenderly. "Don't worry about it. I'll make sure you get your quiet."

I fell in love with him just a little bit more.

* * *

During the final month of my pregnancy, I had a bunch of things I wanted to wrap up before the baby was born. I figured I wouldn't want to do any of it afterwards, so I kept telling the baby, "Not yet, Little One. Mommy's not ready yet."

The most important item on my list was finishing the six-week prenatal belly dance series I'd been attending. I didn't want to miss a single class. Being "so geriatric," I assumed this would be my only pregnancy—and I wanted to extract every possible moment from it.

The other baby makers and I had been learning the graceful, flowing movements of belly dance—hip circles that felt like painting invisible figure eights in the air, gentle undulations that rolled through my spine like ocean waves, and soft swaying that seemed to rock my baby to sleep. The instructor mentioned that belly dancing originated as a way of helping mothers during labor. I could see how the movements encouraged pelvic mobility and helped ease the tension in my lower back and hips. After class, I always felt looser, lighter, and more connected to both my body and the baby.

During class, while I was undulating my hips and circling my arms overhead, my baby would respond with what felt like joyful kicks and wiggles, as if he was dancing along with me in his increasingly cramped little space. I could swear he had his own sense of rhythm.

After class, the baby would usually settle down. The gentle rocking motion, increased oxygen, and my relaxation all seemed to contribute to a sleepy, content baby. I loved the classes, and it seemed my baby did too.

The last class was three days past my due date. My belly button had popped out like a turkey timer; Ryan and I had joked that it meant our baby was officially "done cooking." My skin felt stretched to its absolute limit—like if the baby gained even one more ounce, I might actually pop like a balloon, but I was grateful the baby was still inside so we could attend this final class.

I wrapped the coin-covered belly dance scarf around my hips with practiced ease. The coins chimed softly as I moved—a sound that seemed to echo the flutter of excitement in my chest. As my baby and I swayed and circled for one last time, I felt a bittersweet ache. This was our last prenatal dance together—just the two of us, as we'd been for nine months. This magical phase of carrying him, of being two souls in one body, was about to end forever. Part of me wanted to hold on to this moment, to keep him safe inside me just a little longer.

But as the music faded at the end of class, I knew it was time. I placed my hands on my drum-tight belly, my heart hammering with anticipation and surrender. This was it—after months of "not yet, not yet," I was finally ready to let go.

"Bring it on, Little One. It's time," I whispered to him. The words felt both terrifying and exhilarating.

My baby was listening…

* * *

The next day, Ryan was sitting on the edge of the birthing tub in the tranquil, hotel-like birthing center. I was in the water, squatting in front of him with my arms draped over his thighs, gripping them so tightly I was cutting off his circulation.

Suddenly, he started pushing me off his legs and fully into the tub, saying, "Sorry, Minnie, but I—"

Before I could even register the rudeness of his action, I realized the very legitimate reason—he had passed out and was falling backward. One midwife caught him just in time, cushioning his fall so his head didn't crack open on the tile floor. Crisis averted.

When Ryan came to—looking embarrassed and slightly green around the edges—the midwives force-fed him a banana and some juice before letting him climb back into the tub. Just in time too, because a few minutes later, one final push sent the human watermelon out of me and into the water.

As they handed me my wet and slippery baby, that familiar warm tingle spread through me—the same feeling I'd had during our spiritual conversations. Here was the soul I'd been talking to for months.

The reality of him—warm, breathing, and *here*—hit me like a tidal wave. I was speechless, trembling with emotion for which I had no words. He had been born head down with his hands pressed against his belly just as I'd asked. Our connection had been real.

I met Ryan's eyes and saw the same mixture of awe and love reflected back, for both me and our precious baby.

As we were about to leave the birthing center with four-hour-old Quinn, I suddenly realized he had arrived one month before I turned forty-one.

I had given birth at forty, just as the Spirit had said I would. The timing had been exact, with only a month to spare. It felt like destiny—but it only happened because we said yes, again and again, to the hard choices that got us here. And now Quinn was in my arms.

Chapter 7. A Dysfunctional Family of My Own

I loved having a family of my own. I especially loved being a mother—more than I ever expected, more than anything I had ever loved before.

The first few months after Quinn was born were magical, partly because I felt closer to Ryan than ever before. He was so attentive and helpful—and protective of both Quinn and me. When I struggled with nursing and felt like a complete failure, he didn't just offer empty reassurances. Instead, he contacted my friend who was nursing her older baby and arranged for her to come over and teach me proper positioning and latching techniques. He even completely took over cooking and keeping up the housework so I could get my rest. We were a team, and I loved it.

But slowly, that changed. Maybe it was exhaustion—the bone-deep kind that comes with months of broken sleep. Or maybe it was the way

Ryan retreated back into his video games, staying up later and later, the glow of the screen becoming more familiar to me than his face. The rift between us didn't come all at once—it crept in, quiet and gradual, like fog rolling in from the ocean until suddenly you can't see two feet in front of you.

Maybe Ryan was pulling away because I insisted on keeping Quinn in our bedroom. I couldn't bear to let my baby cry—not even for a minute. Having him right there in his bassinet next to our bed meant I could respond to his first tiny whimper before it escalated into full crying. My body had become completely attuned to him; I'd wake at the slightest sound, heart racing, milk already letting down before I was even fully conscious. I needed my baby close, but Ryan started sleeping in the guest room, claiming Quinn's night sounds kept him awake.

Maybe Ryan pulled away because he thought I was always putting Quinn first. I didn't notice it happening at the time, but I absolutely was. Every decision, every moment of my day revolved around what Quinn needed. But it felt like I was doing it because Ryan was already withdrawing—as if I were filling the space his absence had created.

As my connection with Ryan weakened, my world narrowed to just Quinn. My husband faded more and more into the background. Not deliberately. Not consciously. But it happened all the same.

I convinced myself I was just being a devoted mother—that putting Quinn first was what good mothers do.

However, if I'm brutally honest—and it hurts to admit this—I was also punishing Ryan for not being Sebastian. For not being the partner who would have understood intuitively what I needed, who would have known how to support me without me having to ask.

After the downward spiral began, we became experts at missing each other. If Ryan wanted to talk, I was too tired to form coherent sentences. If he wanted to cuddle, I was always holding the baby or covered in spit-up. If he wanted intimacy—God, even the thought of being touched by anyone else made me want to crawl out of my skin. I told myself it was temporary, just the normal post-baby adjustment period, and that things would eventually balance out. Nonetheless, in the meantime, the distance between us grew wider, and he retreated deeper into his games.

* * *

One day, when Quinn was six months old, I was bustling around the apartment, getting him ready for a trip to the park. I strapped him into his baby wrap, making sure he was bundled against the chilly breeze. His bright eyes followed me as I grabbed a bottle of water and some snacks, double-checking that I had everything. I could already picture the fresh air and the laughter of other kids, and I was eager to feel the sunshine on my face.

But what I really wanted was for Ryan to come with us.

I glanced into the living room where he was hunched over his controller like a stone gargoyle, his attention completely absorbed by the screen where his character was engaged in some epic battle. The familiar sound of explosions and digital gunfire filled the room; it had become the unwelcome soundtrack of our marriage.

"Hey, Ryan," I called, keeping my voice light. "We're heading to the park. Why don't you come with us?"

He didn't even look up. "Can't right now. I'm in the middle of something important."

And there it was. Important—in a way that I clearly wasn't.

I tried to keep the disappointment out of my tone. "It's just a short outing, Ryan. The game can wait."

He sighed, finally setting the controller down and glancing at me. "I'm right in the middle of a big campaign. I'll go another time."

"Fine," I muttered.

I turned away, forcing a smile for Quinn's sake. "Alright, let's go, Little Guy," I murmured.

As I walked away, I heard the familiar sounds of the video game resume as if our conversation had never happened. I felt a surge of rage rise in my chest. I fantasized about replacing his precious gaming chair with an ejector seat that would launch him straight through the ceiling.

Still, I tightened my hold on Quinn and made my way to the door, determined to give my son a day filled with sunshine—even if I had to do it alone.

* * *

A few days later, while I was taking a shower, it hit me like a physical blow—I was married to *Ryan the Gamer*, and I had a *baby*. The steam around me suddenly felt suffocating, the reality crashing down with brutal clarity.

I was trapped. I could *never* leave him now.

My breath came in short, sharp gasps, and my heart hammered so hard against my ribs I thought it might crack them. I wrapped my arms around my chest, trying to hold myself together as I fell apart.

I can't be a single mom. I just can't. The mere thought of it made my stomach lurch with terror. All those warnings from my mom about the horrors of single motherhood came flooding back. I couldn't leave. That meant I was stuck with him—forever—through gaming marathons, emotional distance, or whatever other issues might surface. *No matter what.*

What had I done?

The walls of the small bathroom seemed to pulse inward with each heartbeat, then tilt. My heart pounded louder than the shower spray.

I forced myself to take slower, deeper breaths. I *really* didn't want to pass out in the shower.

I slid down to the shower floor, too dizzy to trust my own legs.

I closed my eyes and counted my breaths, willing the world to stop tilting beneath me.

Everything will be fine.

It had to be.

I repeated it under my breath like a prayer, whispering it whenever my lungs would cooperate.

Everything will be fine.

I *chose* Ryan. Marrying him had been the right choice. We were destined to have a baby. Quinn was here against the odds, so surely it was meant to be. That was the narrative I clung to as the water turned cold around me. I didn't even feel it.

Little by little, the world steadied.

My treacherous mind drifted to Sebastian. No. He was *not* an option. I would *not* let myself go down that path. *Suppress, suppress, suppress…*

Eventually, I realized I was freezing.

As I wrapped myself in a big towel, I kept whispering my new mantra: *Everything will be fine.*

By the time I finished getting dressed and checked on sleeping Quinn, I had almost convinced myself the panic attack had never happened. Everything would be fine—I *had* to believe it. What other choice did I have?

* * *

A month later, when Quinn was seven months old, I was in the bedroom folding baby clothes with Quinn strapped to my chest. Ryan walked in behind me.

"Hey," he said gently. "How come you're still not wearing your wedding ring?"

I didn't look up from the tiny onesie I was folding, my hands suddenly busy smoothing out wrinkles that weren't there. "It doesn't fit yet." My voice came out tighter than I'd intended. It was true, but it wasn't the whole story.

"It could be resized," he said after a pause, his voice carefully neutral. "We could take it in together. Make it fit properly again..." There was something hopeful in his tone, as if he was talking about more than just the ring.

"It'd be a waste of money. I'll just have to resize it again once I lose the baby weight." Again, only part of the story.

The truth was, I just didn't want to wear it. The weight of it on my finger felt wrong now—like a costume from a play I wasn't sure I wanted to be in. I felt guilty for feeling that way, which only made everything worse. I mean, really. What kind of wife doesn't want to wear her wedding ring?

He nodded slowly, but I caught the flicker in his eyes—the pain he tried to hide behind understanding. For a moment, he looked like he might push back—might demand we talk about what was really happening between us. But then his shoulders sagged slightly, and he just walked out of the room.

I was relieved when he left—glad he didn't press, because I didn't want to come up with more half-truths to explain something I didn't fully understand yet. I felt hollow as if I'd failed some test I hadn't known I was taking.

He didn't ask me to wear it again, but something shifted after that. We both felt it, but neither of us mentioned it again.

I hadn't consciously decided to stop wearing the ring, just as I hadn't consciously decided to drift away from him.

* * *

A few weeks later, I was surprised by a text from Sebastian asking for contact information for someone who had gone to graduate school with us. He and I hadn't been in touch for over two years, not since I told him I was getting married.

Hearing from him again made me giddy with delight—my heart skipped as if I were sixteen again. I knew the reaction was completely inappropriate, dangerous even, but I couldn't help it. All those feelings I thought I had successfully buried came rushing back with the force of a dam breaking.

I had been playing peekaboo with Quinn on his favorite blanket, but I immediately scooped him up and deposited him in his rarely used bouncy chair so I could focus entirely on Sebastian's request, as if it couldn't wait another minute.

When Quinn started crying, I ignored him and kept searching for the information.

It was only after I hit send—after Sebastian had thanked me and I'd basked in the warm glow of being helpful to him again—that I realized what I had done. I had ignored my baby's cries for the first time since he was born. I had chosen something—someone—over Quinn.

And it wasn't even my *husband* I'd prioritized. It was my ex-husband. A man who lived halfway across the country and who could never be what I needed. The realization hit me like ice water.

I didn't want to examine what it meant. I just scooped up Quinn and shoved my feelings for Sebastian back into the locked box where they belonged.

However, even as I held my son and promised myself it would never happen again, I decided not to delete Sebastian's number from my phone.

Just in case he needed me again—or I needed him.

* * *

After that, I became more aware of the imbalance I'd created—how my world had narrowed to Quinn alone. I told myself I needed to change that, that I needed to reconnect with Ryan somehow.

I made small, deliberate efforts: looking up when he talked instead of retreating into my phone; sitting beside him on the couch while he played his games, even though the loneliness of being ignored at arm's length made my skin crawl.

Nothing really shifted. And somewhere inside, I was already pulling back—quietly, without drama—letting something essential between us go dark. I was still there physically, still trying, but whatever current we'd once shared no longer reached me.

In the quiet moments when Quinn slept and the house was still, I finally had space to look honestly at what we'd built together. What I saw terrified me.

The only thing anchoring me to the marriage now was Quinn. I wasn't willing to fracture his family before he even had memories of it being whole. So, I stayed—not out of passion or love, but out of responsibility. I stayed because the alternative felt unbearable.

At least, that's the story I told myself as I lay awake in the dark, wondering how we'd drifted so far from where we'd begun.

* * *

A month after the first unexpected text from Sebastian, I received another one. This time, he said he'd be in town on business and would love to catch up over dinner.

I stared at my phone for a long time before responding. I knew I should say no. I knew Ryan wouldn't like it. I knew seeing Sebastian would stir up all the feelings I'd worked hard to bury, feelings that had no place in my married life. I knew I was playing with fire, walking into emotional quicksand.

But I also knew I was going to say yes. The loneliness in my marriage had created a hunger I couldn't ignore, and Sebastian represented everything I was missing—intellectual connection and the feeling of being truly seen. I told myself it was just dinner, just catching up with an old friend. But even as I typed "I'd love to," I knew I was lying to myself about my motivations.

I didn't tell Ryan who I was meeting. I wasn't proud of that.

Bringing Quinn with me was deliberate. I wanted to introduce them. If I was being perfectly honest, I wanted to experience—however briefly—what family life could have been like with Sebastian. Apparently, I enjoyed torturing myself.

Sebastian looked like he had just stepped out of a GQ photo shoot. His gorgeousness made me highly self-conscious about being a frumpy mom, but he didn't seem to notice. He still looked at me as if I was the most fascinating person ever. How could I resist that?

"Oh my goodness, Minnie," he said softly, crouching down to Quinn's eye level. "He's absolutely beautiful. The photos on Facebook don't capture how alert and bright he is." He gently touched Quinn's tiny hand. "Hello there, Little Fellow."

Quinn responded with a delighted gurgle.

Watching them, I felt a pang of longing I wasn't ready to examine too closely. "Thanks, Sebastian." I settled Quinn into a highchair to distract myself from the sudden resurgence of carefully suppressed, entirely inappropriate feelings.

As we waited for our server, Sebastian's attention remained completely focused on Quinn. He was making silly faces and gentle cooing sounds that drew delighted giggles from my son. "He has that same curious expression you get when you're taking everything in," Sebastian said, glancing up at me with that familiar warmth.

He would have been an amazing dad. Stop it.

He turned his attention to me. "Tell me about your life. How are you balancing work with being a new mom? That must be quite the juggling act." Our taboo against speaking about our relationships was still in place, but we found plenty of topics to discuss for the next hour, and I felt connected to another person in a way I hadn't in a long time.

As we said goodbye, Sebastian held me close. "You know I'm always here if you need anything, don't you? Just a phone call away. I mean that."

I teared up at his words because I knew he truly meant them. That was the problem.

As I drove home, the contrast between the evening I'd just had and the life waiting for me felt almost unbearable.

* * *

I knew it wasn't fair to compare Ryan to Sebastian. Part of me even realized I was comparing the worst, most frustrating moments with Ryan against carefully curated memories of my ex. But knowing it wasn't fair didn't stop the thoughts from creeping in, no matter how unwanted they were.

Over the next few months, I continued to feel disconnected from Ryan, and the contrast with that one evening with Sebastian just made everything worse. That dinner had reminded me of the type of connection I no longer had.

The distance between us continued to grow, like a chasm I couldn't cross, and I was getting more miserable by the day. The thought of living this way indefinitely—feeling isolated while being married, going through the motions of partnership while feeling completely alone—terrified me as much as the thought of actually being single.

I felt caught between impossible alternatives: stay in a marriage that was slowly suffocating me, or become the single mother I had sworn I'd never be. Neither path felt survivable, but standing still was becoming unbearable, too.

* * *

I woke suddenly to a burst of laughter. It took a moment for my groggy mind to catch up. For a moment, I lay still, letting my eyes adjust to the bright afternoon sun pouring rudely into the room.

There it was again—genuine, carefree laughter. It had been so long since I'd heard that sound in our house that it took me a second to recognize it. When was the last time Ryan had laughed like that with me? I couldn't remember.

Ryan and his three teenagers were joking around in the kitchen. They were visiting for a week and clearly having a great time.

They always seemed to laugh more when I wasn't with them.

I understood—I was the stepmother they barely knew, just the latest woman attached to their dad, someone they occasionally visited but never belonged to. But Ryan… what was his excuse?

"Dad, can we go get ice cream?" Sarah asked.

His son jumped at the suggestion. "Yeah! And we can give Quinn his first taste of ice cream! Minnie's super strict about that stuff, but she's not here…"

Ryan chuckled—actually chuckled—and he sounded so genuinely happy when he answered. "You know what? Great idea. Quinn will love having his own little cone. What she doesn't know won't hurt her, right?"

Oh, yeah. Great idea. Side with your kids instead of your wife.

Then, he continued lower and more serious, "Shhh, don't wake her up. This can be our little secret. She needs her rest anyway."

It wasn't that Quinn could never have ice cream. We were still introducing foods to him, one at a time, to check for allergies. Why did that make me the enemy?

I understood that Ryan rarely saw his kids and wanted to maximize bonding time when they visited. This wasn't just about time with his kids, though. This was about him being a completely different person when I wasn't around—warmer, more spontaneous, and more fun. The father and man I'd hoped he could be with Quinn and me, but wasn't anymore.

I stayed in bed, hearing the front door open and close, their voices and laughter fading into the distance.

I lay there, a bit stunned. I felt betrayed.

It wasn't about the ice cream at all.

I couldn't help but wonder if Ryan even wanted to spend time with me anymore. We didn't really connect—we coexisted, mostly talking logistics. It was not what either of us wanted.

By the time the front door opened again, I still felt raw and vulnerable, but I pushed those feelings down. I went to greet them, determined to keep things pleasant.

"Hey, did you have a good time?" I asked, summoning a smile I didn't feel.

"It was great!" Sarah said brightly. "Quinn had so much fun at the park."

The park. Right. I looked at Quinn, searching for telltale signs of ice cream—sticky fingers, a chocolate smudge. Nothing. They'd been thorough in covering their tracks.

Ryan nodded, holding Quinn, who giggled and babbled happily in his arms. Probably from a sugar rush. "Yeah, it was a nice break," he said, not meeting my eyes.

A break—from what, exactly?

I swallowed my bitter thoughts and nodded, keeping my smile in place. "I'm glad you had fun," I managed, my voice sounding hollow even to my own ears. I turned away before my smile cracked.

* * *

I tolerated the rest of my step kids' visit. Then I tolerated the next few weeks. I wondered how long I would have to tolerate my life. I kept telling myself things would get better, that Ryan and I would laugh and talk again someday, that the loneliness was just temporary.

But eventually, I knew I couldn't tolerate it anymore. Something had to change. My fingers hovered over my laptop's keyboard.

Leave? Stay? The question had been haunting me for weeks. My parents had already said Quinn and I were welcome anytime, no questions asked. Leaving didn't have to mean ending my marriage—I was just taking space to breathe.

There really was no choice. I couldn't stand it anymore. I needed a break. I closed my eyes and took a deep, steadying breath.

Yes. I need this.

I sat frozen, staring at the screen for a long moment.

Then I clicked *Confirm Booking* for the one-way tickets.

I didn't know how long the break would need to be, but Quinn and I would leave the next day, expensive last-minute ticket prices be damned.

As I packed, my thoughts swirled. How did we let our relationship fall so far? How could we have become such strangers to each other? I'd been terrified of becoming a single mother, but I already felt like one while Ryan retreated into work and his video games.

I knew I was also to blame for our relationship falling apart. Knowing that didn't tell me how to fix it, however.

I hoped a break would bring clarity and shake us out of the downward spiral.

Ryan opened the bedroom door, his brown eyes immediately finding the open suitcase on our bed like a neon sign announcing disaster. His whole body went still. "What's going on? Are we going somewhere?"

We? It hadn't felt like a "we" in months. Hearing him call us that actually stung.

"Not exactly…" It would have been easier to slip out into the night, but I couldn't do that to him. I could at least be mature enough to tell him. "Quinn and I are going to visit my parents. I, uh, booked a one-way ticket."

My tone of voice, more than the words, let Ryan know this was more than just a visit. He stepped backward in shock and hurt. I don't know why he was surprised. Couldn't he feel the distance between us?

"Why?" he asked, and for the first time in weeks, I heard real emotion in his voice—not the flat, distracted tone he used when discussing logistics, but actual hurt and confusion.

I looked down at the tiny clothes I was folding—outfits I'd bought when I still believed our family life would be everything I'd dreamed. "I just need some space… from this… from us." The words tasted like failure.

I felt like a terrible wife. And maybe a bad mother.

Ryan didn't say anything right away. I could feel his gaze on my back, but I couldn't bring myself to look at him.

"I can't believe you're doing this," he said, his voice cracking slightly. "Taking my son away from me." He knew exactly which words would cut deepest.

"I'm sorry…" I began, but he cut me off.

"You should have said something. We should have talked about this."

And now the blame. *When was I supposed to say something? Between your gaming sessions?* I kept folding Quinn's tiny socks and said nothing.

He eventually walked away, huffing in anger.

I sighed and zipped the suitcase closed with more force than necessary. I had no idea what would happen next—whether this break would save us or end us. I only knew I couldn't breathe in this house anymore, and I couldn't pretend we were okay for one more day.

Chapter 8. No More Chasing Rainbows

Being at my parents' house was a relief in ways I hadn't anticipated. Mom asked a lot of questions—about Quinn, about Ryan and me, and about what had brought us there—which reminded me of how starved I'd been for that kind of attention. Ryan hadn't asked much of anything in a long time. Mom's questions weren't about fixing me or pushing for answers; they were simply a way of saying, *I see you. I care about you.*

I envied their well-oiled partnership after forty-five years of marriage. They'd figured out something essential that Ryan and I were clearly missing—*how to be individuals within a unit.* Mom loved her kitchen, which Dad had remodeled for her a few years earlier, so much that she shooed everyone else out and did all the cooking. Dad had his workshop sanctuary, where the sound of his tools provided a comforting background soundtrack, and Mom never interfered with his projects.

And yet they also chose each other—settling in to watch their evening shows, visiting friends together, or sharing a comfortable silence over breakfast. They had mastered something that felt impossibly out of reach to me: being both independent and connected. Ryan and I weren't connected, but we weren't truly independent either. We were just… existing in parallel.

They absolutely loved having Quinn there. After years of watching my siblings' kids grow up from a distance, this felt like a precious second chance for them to really know a grandchild. Far from feeling like an imposition, I could see how much joy his presence brought them.

In their house, I didn't have to pretend to be okay. For the first time in a long while, I felt held.

That sense of safety gave me the space to really look at my situation. Should I leave Ryan? Go back to him?

I knew I couldn't stay suspended in this protective bubble forever. I'd spent weeks analyzing every possible outcome—building mental pros-and-cons lists, talking myself into and out of every option—until I was dizzy with indecision. No amount of rational thought could untangle the knot I was trapped in.

I needed clarity—something beyond my own overthinking, or even talking things through with Mom.

That's when I decided to try Reiki. I didn't know much about it, only that it was a form of energy work—something similar to what Ryan and I had explored early in our relationship. Maybe it would shake something loose.

It was worth trying.

* * *

The Reiki master I found was a wiry man in his late fifties with thinning gray hair tied back in a low ponytail. His studio had crystals clustered on every available surface, sandalwood incense wafting through the room, and soft meditation music playing from hidden speakers. He looked legit.

"I'm feeling really stuck," I began.

"No need," he said, interrupting me. "You don't need to tell me anything—your energy will tell me everything I need to know."

Well, that sounded promising.

After twenty minutes of staring at the inside of my eyelids, however, I was getting mad. Nothing was happening. I was lying on his massage table, and he was doing literally nothing. His hands rested on my shoulders, but they weren't moving at all. I didn't feel any energy shifting, pulsing, or buzzing—nothing.

Ryan could move energy, and he'd learned how in a two-hour workshop.

That's when it occurred to me that this man might not be a healer at all, but a scam artist with a fancy, spiritual-looking studio designed to convince seekers like me to pay *five freaking dollars a minute*—yes, *$300 an hour*—for the most expensive nap of their lives. I realized I should have asked to see credentials before handing my credit card to this quack.

Just as I was about to give up and see if I could get a refund, I felt a sensation in my chest that hadn't been there before. First, it was just a small tingling sensation in my heart chakra, as if a butterfly had landed on my chest. Then it spread outward—down my arms and legs, up into my head—like liquid lightning, until every cell felt alive and buzzing. The tingle got stronger until it was like electricity zapping through me, especially around my heart. It was disturbing. As the zapping sensation continued, my body started jerking involuntarily, as if he had attached me to an electrical stimulation unit and turned it up too high.

As I freaked out emotionally and spazzed out physically, the Reiki master calmly kept his hands on my shoulders, as if this were normal. Would falling off the table be normal? I was afraid that was going to happen, and I'd be unable to stop it.

Then I felt something new—my heart chakra literally opening, like a tightly closed rosebud blooming in a fast-forward time lapse. I could see it in my mind's eye: a luminous red rose unfolding petal by petal in the center of my chest.

But as it opened fully, something in my gut lurched. The flower's center was full of black sludge—sour and rotting—like something long stagnant, suddenly stirred up.

As the rose opened, the black sludge began to bubble, slowly at first, like lava coming to a boil. The bubbles grew larger and more violent until the sludge spilled over, pouring out of the rose and creeping down the sides of my body, dripping into pools of ick on the floor.

Throughout the vision, I thrashed on the table like a wild woman. The Reiki master didn't react. He simply kept his hands on my shoulders, steady as a rock, channeling energy as whatever needed to leave finally did.

Eventually, the last of the blackness drained away. What remained was an open rose—red, emptied, and exposed to its core. I collapsed back onto the table, utterly spent.

My body felt like lead, and my heart felt scraped clean and hollow—but in the most relieving way possible. Something enormous had been released, and even though I had no idea what it was, I felt lighter than I had in years.

The Reiki master kept his hands on my shoulders for a few more minutes, then slowly got up.

"Take all the time you need," he said softly as he stepped quietly out of the room, leaving me alone with the aftermath.

I stared up at the ceiling, too tired to get up. All I could do was lie there and wonder—*What the hell was that?*

* * *

When I went to bed that night, I still didn't know what the black sludge meant. I must have understood it subconsciously, though, because its meaning came out in a dream.

I was standing in what had once been a magnificent ballroom—the kind of place where fairy tale weddings had happened. But now it was a ruin of its former self.

The once-gleaming hardwood floor was warped and splintered beneath my feet, while strips of wallpaper sagged from the walls. The crystal chandeliers that had once sparkled with light were now clouded with dust, with many of their crystals missing like broken teeth.

As I took in the heartbreaking decay, someone tapped my shoulder, and I turned to find Sebastian standing there. Even in this ruined place, seeing him filled me with familiar warmth, that sense of coming home. He smiled at me with the same tender expression I remembered, as if no time had passed, as if nothing had ever gone wrong between us. He took me into his arms and just held me, and I reveled in the feeling.

The floor began to tremble beneath our feet, gently at first, then with increasing violence. The damaged chandeliers swayed dangerously overhead, and their remaining crystals started chiming like broken church bells. Chunks of ornate ceiling plaster began raining down around us. Other people in the ballroom—people I hadn't noticed before—screamed and ran for the exits.

I tried to turn, to pull us toward safety, but Sebastian planted his feet like an anchor. "Come on, we have to get out of here!" I screamed over the sound of cracking walls and falling debris. Instead of running, he tightened his arms around me, holding me firmly against his chest.

"No," he said, his voice strangely calm despite the chaos. "Stay with me."

I fought against his embrace, panic rising as the building shuddered around us. "Sebastian, please! The whole place is coming down!" He only held me tighter.

Just before a massive section of ceiling crashed down on us, I heard a tremendous THUD from somewhere in the real world, yanking me violently out of the nightmare.

I bolted upright, heart hammering, my nightgown soaked with sweat. For a moment, I could still feel the phantom pressure of Sebastian's arms around me and hear the sound of the ballroom collapsing.

Then I noticed a sound coming from the closet. Something was moving in there.

As much as I wanted to throw the blanket over my head and ignore it, I knew I wouldn't be able to fall back asleep if I didn't find out what it was. I carefully opened the door, hoping nothing would jump out at me.

Remnants of my past with Sebastian came spilling out onto the floor—things I hadn't been able to part with but didn't think I should keep in the home I shared with Ryan.

Tucked away on the top shelf of my parents' guest room closet for years, hidden from view but never truly forgotten, were my old wedding album, the box containing my first wedding dress, and a box of our wedding memorabilia—invites, table decorations, my silk bouquet. They had all, somehow, just fallen to the floor.

I stood there shivering in my nightgown, staring at the scattered remnants of my first marriage spread across the floor. The timing was impossible to ignore—the Reiki session, the dream, and now this.

The message landed with brutal clarity—I couldn't keep dragging the ruins of one life into the next.

* * *

The nightmare shook me to my core and reminded me I had never really let Sebastian go—not the man, and certainly not what he represented.

It had been eight years since we separated. I'd assumed time would have done its work by now. It hadn't.

Instead of grieving, I'd kept moving. Dating. Replacing. Convincing myself that if I stayed in motion, the ache would dissolve on its own.

If I wanted any kind of future—whether with Ryan or on my own—I had to stop carrying the past into it.

I needed to let Sebastian go.

* * *

I decided to try a New Age "cut-the-cord" ceremony. I sat cross-legged on the floor with determination like some New Age warrior princess preparing for battle. It seemed ironic, since Sebastian had been the one who introduced me to New Age beliefs.

I closed my eyes and visualized Sebastian sitting across from me. His heartwarming baby blue eyes materialized in my mind, making my heart skip a beat even in imagination. *Great start. Nothing says "letting go" quite like getting lost in my ex's imaginary eyes.*

Forging ahead, I focused on my root chakra, and I imagined a glowing red cord extending from it to Sebastian's root chakra. Next, I connected our sacral chakras with an orange cord, our solar plexus with yellow, heart with green, throat with blue, third eye with indigo, and finally our crown chakras with white. We were linked by a beautiful, shimmering rainbow of energy. I snorted. The rainbow felt on-the-nose—my brain will crack a joke at the worst possible time.

My trouble staying focused was probably a clue I really didn't want to "cut the cord" with him, but I forced myself to continue. It *needed* to happen.

I started the exchange. I mentally sent memories, emotions, and Sebastian-flavored beliefs across the cords. I definitely discarded the idea that I was sexually broken. He hadn't given me that belief outright, but years of rejection—and him deciding he was gay while married to me—had made me feel fundamentally defective.

Back and forth it went until I felt like I had taken back all of me and given back all of him.

It was time to do the cutting. I raised my hands above my head and paused for just a moment. I braced myself. *This needs to be done.* With a swift and decisive motion, I brought my hands slicing down in front of me, intending to cut through the energetic ties once and for all.

But, fuck! The pain hit me like a freight train. It felt like my arms popped out of their sockets, then went back in.

The cords connecting us were still *far* too strong to be cut. I had turned Sebastian into an ideal, and ideals are harder to let go of than real people.

I realized the sad truth—I was nowhere near ready to let go of *Saint Sebastian*, no matter how much I knew I should.

Shit. What am I going to do? Am I doomed to be haunted by memories of him, by my connection to him, forever?

I realized I couldn't do this by myself. I needed professional help again. More Reiki might have been a good idea, but I didn't want to spend so much money this time, so I looked for other options.

I wondered how I would explain to my next therapist that invisible black goo, a spooky nightmare, and a botched New Age ritual led to an epiphany about needing therapy, without sounding like I'd completely lost my marbles.

* * *

I scoured the internet until I found someone who I thought could help me and discovered an "emotional release therapist." She claimed to "tap into the body's innate wisdom to uncover and release buried trauma, guiding the process with gentle, nonverbal techniques."

That sounded perfect because I knew speaking would become difficult for me when we started getting into it.

During our session, she walked me through something called "ideomotor signaling"—a fancy way of saying move my index finger for "yes," my pinky finger for "no." With my hand resting on my chest and my eyes closed, she began her detective work.

"Can we release something today?" My index finger moved. Yes.

She narrowed in like a heat-seeking missile. "Is it related to Sebastian?" Yes.

"Is it about the end of your marriage?" Yes.

"Is it guilt?"

How could it not be? What I did was despicable. Yes.

"Can you release it?"

Pause. *I don't deserve to release it.* I lifted my pinky. No.

She continued asking questions, slowly chipping away at the underlying issues, helping me release layer after layer of guilt and shame I'd been wearing like a medieval hair shirt.

Finally: "Can you release all of this now?"

This time, my index finger rose on its own before I had time to argue with it. Yes.

I exhaled a long, cleansing breath—and promptly burst into tears of relief.

* * *

Afterwards, I wasn't suddenly over Sebastian, but the soul-crushing shame about how I'd ended our marriage was finally gone. That alone felt enormous.

I didn't know whether that shift was energetic, psychological, or just grief finally getting bored and packing up its bags. Maybe something had actually been released. Maybe I'd just stopped flogging myself for the same old crime. Either way, I no longer felt stuck in the past, waiting for Sebastian—or some romanticized version of that life—to come back and save me.

I felt ready to move forward, even if I still had no idea what forward was supposed to look like.

* * *

Over the next few days, my guilt for taking Quinn away from Ryan grew. He and I had been in touch every few days, so I knew how much he was missing both of us—but especially Quinn.

During our video calls with Ryan, Quinn would press his chubby hands against the laptop screen and babble urgently, as if trying to climb through to reach his daddy. Each time the screen went dark when the call ended, he looked at me with those big eyes that broke my heart; it was as if he was asking, "Where did Daddy go?"

Quinn was getting close to walking—six weeks was a long time in a baby's development—and if I didn't go home soon, Ryan would miss his first steps. I would have been *furious* if Ryan had left with Quinn. *Why had I convinced myself it was okay to take him away?*

Now that I was beginning to untangle my unresolved feelings for Sebastian, I felt even guiltier for leaving. A lot of our problems, heck maybe even most of them, stemmed from grief I'd never fully addressed. Something Ryan had no control over. That was on me.

I saw that as a good thing. I convinced myself that if I were the problem, I could fix it.

Now that my heart was (more) free from Sebastian, I hoped I could finally show up fully in my marriage in a way I hadn't been able to before.

I wanted to.

Not because I was wildly in love with Ryan—not in the way I had once hoped to be—but because I wanted our family to stay together. Because I wanted Quinn to grow up with both of his parents under the same roof. More than anything, I couldn't bear the thought of split custody—the idea of being away from my baby for even a single night felt intolerable.

Deep down, I didn't really want to lose Ryan either. He wasn't a bad person. He was a good person with bad coping mechanisms. And I hadn't always been easy to live with lately, either.

I hadn't told him how isolated I'd felt. I hadn't told him how often I cried in the shower so he wouldn't hear me. I hadn't told him how scared I was that we were turning into two ships passing in the night.

Maybe if I stopped expecting him to be a straight Sebastian, and he stopped punishing himself for not being enough, we could still build something out of what was left between us.

Watching my parents over these weeks had reminded me what a healthy partnership could look like. They had separate interests, but they also chose each other intentionally. They'd figured out how to be individuals within their marriage without drifting into strangers.

Maybe Ryan and I could learn that balance, too. Maybe we could find our way to something like what my parents had built.

It was worth trying for. It had to be.

At least, that was the hope I clung to as I packed our bags and prepared to return home.

Chapter 9. Honey, I Shrunk the Income

I was glad I went back.

After the torment he had been through when I left, Ryan was just as committed as I was to rebuilding our marriage into something stronger and more satisfying than it had been. We worked through a save-your-marriage program—weekly exercises, awkward check-in questions, and long conversations we'd avoided for years. It was working.

We were finally listening to each other. I opened up and let him in again, and he really tried to meet me where I was.

I felt seen again. He felt appreciated again. We built new routines and healed some of the old wounds. It felt like our love was regrowing. I let myself hope our marriage could be truly fulfilling.

Our family life was back on track, too. The tension that used to fill our house had lifted, and it was more like the warm haven I'd always wanted it to be. Now that Quinn was walking, we created a favorite new game: "I'm gonna get you." We would chase him around the house and not quite catch him. He would squeal in delight, and Ryan and I would share a warm look over his head.

Things weren't perfect, but they finally felt livable.

* * *

One afternoon, six months after I returned, I was washing dishes when Ryan got home from work.

"Hey," I said, glancing at the clock. "You're home early."

He sighed and ran a hand through his hair. "Yeah… HR handed out walking papers today. Mine too. Whole thing was a total suckorama."

I froze.

He had brought it up the week before—half-joking, or so I'd thought. He'd been in charge of choosing three people to lay off from his department in a company-wide cut. After picking the first two, he said he couldn't bring himself to choose a third. He said maybe he should just put his own name down.

I hadn't just said no; I'd said *"Hell, no!"*

We couldn't afford that. I was only consulting part-time because of taking care of Quinn. We needed the stability his job provided.

I thought he'd heard me. I thought he *agreed* with me.

But no. So now he was unemployed—and in that moment, all I could see was stupidity, although he undoubtedly saw it as noble—sacrificing himself instead of someone else.

"You actually did it?" I asked, already knowing the answer.

He nodded. "I couldn't do it, Minnie. Those guys have kids. Mortgages. The whole nine yards. I couldn't be the guy who wrecked another family."

I stared at him. My stomach dropped; I was afraid I was going to be sick. But the fear was quickly overtaken by fury.

"And *you* don't?" I said, my voice barely more than a whisper. "*We're* not a family?"

"Hey, that's not what I meant. Don't make me the bad guy here."

I couldn't believe it. I would wake up and find out this was a bad dream—because he couldn't possibly be so irresponsible in real life.

"Look, it's not like I didn't think about us. I got a good severance package, and I'll start looking right away. I just… I couldn't do it any other way."

My brain spun. We'd built our life around him keeping this job—and he knew it. We had agreed—together—that he'd carry us financially for a few years, so I could focus on our son. I thought we were a team. Teams don't make decisions like this unilaterally.

Instead, he'd made a massive choice on his own, tossing our stability—and my trust—aside in a single moment.

Ryan had stopped talking at some point and was waiting for a response, but I still didn't know what to say.

Quinn toddled in just then. He raised his arms to be picked up. "Da-da," he said brightly.

I scooped him up, pressing my cheek to his soft hair, trying to stay calm.

Ryan smiled faintly and ruffled Quinn's hair. "At least somebody's still happy to see me."

I finally met his gaze, my expression flat. "We'll figure something out," I managed.

What I really wanted to say was:

What the fuck were you thinking?

* * *

A year later, he *still* hadn't found a new job. I wondered what he was really doing when he claimed to be looking for jobs. Actually, I was pretty sure the answer involved digital quests, and if I gave it much thought, it pissed me off.

During that year, we'd moved from Portland to rural Ohio—closer to my parents, with a much lower cost of living that helped stretch my part-time consulting income. Even so, we were barely staying afloat.

Now his unemployment had run out and our savings were gone. It was clear I needed to step up.

My plan had been to ramp up my career when Quinn started school at five. This was two-and-a-half years ahead of schedule. I wasn't ready, but readiness was no longer relevant.

I told myself my reluctance to rebuild my business was about motherhood and exhaustion. That was only part of the truth. The deeper reason was one I could never admit to Ryan—because it led straight back to Sebastian.

My career had always been intertwined with him. We'd met in graduate school, built our careers side by side, and eventually launched a consulting business together. It had been *ours*.

After our marriage ended, he moved on. I bought him out. On paper, the business was mine. In my heart, it still echoed with *us*—what we'd built, what we'd imagined, what never came to be.

As long as I focused on Quinn instead of work, I could keep those echoes buried.

But avoidance is a luxury you lose when the bills come due.

It didn't matter if I wasn't ready. It didn't matter if expanding my business meant reopening old wounds. I had to provide for my family.

So, with conflicted emotions and a tightness in my chest I tried to ignore, I decided it was time to put myself back out there.

I would start going to conferences again to drum up business. I worried what would happen to our dynamic if I became the primary provider—but it was no longer a choice. I would pick up the slack, even though that meant secretly grappling with my memories of Sebastian.

* * *

A month later, I walked into the opening session of my first conference back—a meet-and-greet. I dreaded sessions like this because I'm such an introvert, but in consulting, visibility is survival.

I scanned the room, looking for a familiar face.

And then, out of nowhere, there he was.

Sebastian.

He was laughing and talking to a group of people. He shone in situations like this. It was one of the many ways we had fit so well together—he was great at schmoozing and finding work, and I was great at getting the work done.

He was wearing a perfectly tailored business suit that made him look both effortlessly polished and infuriatingly gorgeous—more distinguished than I'd ever seen him. All my old feelings for him flooded my system. I'd released some of my attachment to him in that session a year and a half ago—but there was clearly plenty left.

What was he doing here, anyway? He had never attended this conference before—at least, not that I knew of.

I had known I would have to confront my feelings about Sebastian as part of building up my consulting business, but I hadn't thought I'd have to do it *in his presence.* I had thought I'd just be wrestling with memories, and at least most of the time, I could distract myself with other things.

But seeing him in person—at a conference like we used to attend together? That was firing old neural pathways like crazy. It was as if we had never been apart, like one of us had simply been away on an extended business trip, and now we were finally back where we belonged.

I don't know how long I stared. Suddenly, as if he could feel me staring, he turned—and his eyes locked onto mine.

First, surprise. Then, delight.

I didn't think. I just moved.

"Minnie? Wow… it's been a long time." He smiled, a little surprised but warm. "It's really good to see you here. I'm glad you're still in the game."

Hugging him felt so right—like a mistake had finally been corrected: we were still married and all the years apart had been nothing but a bad dream.

I had no idea what we talked about—I was too wrapped up in the sheer joy of being near him again. He smelled so damn good, like his expensive shampoo I used to smell on my pillowcase—like home, despite everything. Being with him was an unexpected gift.

As the session ended, Sebastian smiled and said, "I'd love to catch up properly. Want to grab lunch tomorrow?"

"I'd love to," I heard myself agreeing before my rational mind could intervene.

What the hell am I doing?

I stood there, stunned by my own behavior. I had just agreed to have lunch with Sebastian—to reopen something that needed to stay shut down—without even thinking it through.

This was exactly what I shouldn't be doing. I was married, trying to rebuild with Ryan—and here I was making plans with the one person who could unravel all of it.

But God, it felt so good to see him again. To feel that spark of recognition, that sense of being truly seen by someone who knew me so completely.

If Sebastian had asked, I would have left Ryan in a heartbeat. The thought was absurd, irrational, and impossible—and yet the desire burned all the same.

I had thought I'd buried my feelings for Sebastian, but clearly not. I needed to focus on Ryan—on my marriage, on my son.

But not yet.

Just lunch. That was all.

I would allow myself to bask in Sebastian's company, to soak in the comfort of his presence, for a few precious hours.

Then, after I returned home, I'd pretend it hadn't stirred anything at all, and I'd try—once again—to push my feelings back underground.

* * *

I couldn't let my feelings about Sebastian paralyze me—our family's survival depended on me pushing through the discomfort and getting back out there professionally.

A few more conferences helped kick-start my consulting business. At first, every trip stirred memories of Sebastian, and I caught myself scanning the crowd for him. But he never appeared.

Over time, the memories faded, replaced by new ones. And slowly, other parts of my life began to fill in again.

One good thing that happened during this time was Ryan and I started teaching ballroom dance lessons together. I had stopped teaching partway through my pregnancy, and I missed it. When I heard the local arts center was looking for someone to teach, I jumped at it. Ryan came to most of my classes, and before long, we were teaching as a team.

We also took Quinn with us, and he would play with his trucks during class, happily absorbed in his own small world.

What surprised me most was how naturally Ryan could explain the man's role. During one tango lesson, I was struggling to help a male student understand the concept of leading without being pushy. I watched Ryan step in, his voice calm and clear.

"Okay, here's how I think of it. You're offering an invitation," he said, demonstrating with his partner. "You're not dragging her where you want to go. You're suggesting a direction with your frame, then giving her space to accept and follow. The connection happens in that moment when she feels your intention and decides to trust it."

I stared at him, impressed despite myself. In all my years of teaching, I'd never articulated it quite that way. He had thought more deeply about the dynamics of partnering than I'd ever realized. Watching him guide the student through the steps, I felt a flutter of attraction I hadn't experienced in months. The last time I'd felt that way about him seemed like a lifetime ago. This thoughtful, articulate man—where had he been hiding?

The best part, though, was the Nutcracker performance—specifically, the two adult numbers I had choreographed. I didn't work with the children in the production, but the ballroom sequences were mine. I had shaped them, staged them, drilled them until the timing felt effortless.

Ryan had agreed to step into the shoes of the grandfather—a role that demanded not just dance skill but comedic timing. No one else was willing to take the role, so I'd asked Ryan to step up. I was grateful—and nervous. He'd never performed on stage before, and the role required acting instincts he'd never tested in front of an audience.

Backstage, while I paced and mentally ran through counts and cues, Ryan stood in costume adjusting his vest with surprising calm.

"You're going to be great," I whispered, squeezing his hand.

He winked at me. "I know," he said with a grin that made my stomach flip.

During the performance, I watched him hobble onto the stage with exaggerated frailty, leaning heavily on his cane. The audience chuckled at his first shuffling steps, but when the maid grabbed his shoulders, planted a foot against his back, and gave an over-the-top "adjustment" that sent him lurching upright with a comedic crack, Ryan instantly straightened, tossed the cane aside, and swept her into a waltz that was both graceful and hilarious.

His performance was impeccable. Every gesture and expression landed perfectly. When the waltz ended with Ryan feigning his bad back returning, "dropping" the maid unceremoniously on the floor during the final dip, and hobbling off with his cane, the applause was thunderous.

I was genuinely stunned. This confident, magnetic performer—this was my husband? He had just commanded the stage as if he'd been doing it for years.

As he disappeared into the wings, slightly out of breath and beaming, I felt something I hadn't experienced in ages: pure, uncomplicated attraction to the man I'd married.

That night, I wanted him.

* * *

But the confidence he showed on stage didn't carry over into the rest of his life. He ended up with a string of part-time, minimum-wage jobs—first an elementary school teacher's assistant, then a lifeguard, and finally a grocery store clerk. He never said it outright, but I could see what it did to him. The way his shoulders slumped when he left for work. The way he avoided telling people what he did. He felt like a failure who couldn't support his family, and that shame seeped into everything.

I couldn't see it then, but Ryan's increasing depression about unemployment was directly feeding his escapism into games, which drove my withdrawal. We were in a feedback loop neither of us understood and neither of us knew how to escape.

I tried to be supportive—I really did. I encouraged him and suggested new directions he could take. But he resented my suggestions. It wasn't the kind of support he wanted, and I didn't know how to give the kind he did want.

Our marriage suffered. His disappointment in himself and my growing resentment hung in the space between us. We drifted apart. We barely touched. Most conversations were about logistics. We felt more like roommates than partners—bound by responsibility rather than love.

I didn't know how much longer we could go on like that. I didn't want to be a single mom, even though it would be easier now that Quinn was older. I still wanted my marriage to work, though. Just sometimes, it felt so hopeless.

The constant stress about money also wore me down. I enjoyed consulting, but it was feast or famine, and I never knew if I'd make enough money to pay the bills the next month. I craved more stability—especially if things weren't going to last with Ryan.

So, when I came across a job posting that looked promising, I knew exactly what I needed to do.

I needed to call Sebastian.

* * *

The job sounded perfect for me. It was similar to the work I was already doing, but with a steady paycheck and benefits—and I'd still get to work from home. It almost seemed too good to be true, so I wanted inside information to be sure.

I hesitated before dialing, my finger hovering over Sebastian's name on my phone screen. I wasn't sure if he'd answer—or if this was still his number. It had been five years since we'd last spoken. Out of everyone I knew, though, he still seemed like the best person to talk to about this. He knew the owners of the company, as well as the industry. Most importantly, he knew *me.*

It was the right thing to do. I placed the call.

He answered right away. "Well, this is a nice surprise. You caught me off guard—in the best way." My nervousness about calling him faded away upon hearing his warm greeting. It was good to hear his voice.

"Hey, Sebastian. I was hoping to get the inside scoop on a job I'm considering."

He listened as I explained the job posting—my concerns about going from being an independent consultant to a full-time employee—and my uncertainty about working for someone else again. I half-expected him to poke fun at me, to remind me I'd always sworn I'd never go back to corporate life.

Instead, he said, "You'd be perfect for this, and I think you'd really enjoy it."

I was pleased to hear that. "You really think so?"

"I do. The owners are solid people—smart, ethical, and grounded. Not easy to find these days. And they've built a culture you'll actually want to be part of." He paused, and then added, "If you decide to make the leap, I'm confident it'll be a good one."

I exhaled, the tension I hadn't even realized I was holding starting to ease. "That's… really good to hear."

We talked a bit after that about safe topics—mainly work and family members. The conversation flowed easily, but something felt different this time. I couldn't quite put my finger on what it was.

When we hung up, I was confident about the job opportunity—and strangely peaceful about everything else. I waited for the familiar emotional aftershock. It never came.

I still cared about him, but the deep longing was gone. It felt odd, disappointing even, that I had finally let go without realizing it. It was bittersweet, but freeing all the same. I just never expected it to take fifteen years.

* * *

"I got the job!" I announced as I walked out of my home office a week later, still buzzing with excitement from the phone call with my new employer.

Ryan looked up from his laptop at the kitchen table, where he'd been "job searching"—though the gaming website still open in his browser tab suggested otherwise.

"That's great," he said, flashing a quick smile that didn't quite reach his eyes. "Really great. We needed this."

"The salary is more than we made combined last year," I said, unable to contain my relief and pride. "And it comes with great benefits."

"Wow." He closed the laptop. "Look at you, keeping us in the fancy groceries now." He tried for a grin, but it flickered and died almost as soon as it appeared. "So, you'll be working full-time then?"

"Yes, but from home mostly. Same as consulting, just… steady."

He nodded, running a hand through his hair—a gesture I'd come to recognize as his way of processing something uncomfortable. "That's… that's really good, Minnie. I'm happy for you. For us."

There was a pause, and in it, I could feel all the things he wasn't saying. That I'd succeeded where he'd failed. That I was now officially our family's provider. That his role—whatever it had been—had just shrunk again.

"Ryan—"

"No, really," he said quickly, standing up from the table. "This is exactly what we needed. You crushed it. I'm proud of you." But as he moved past me toward the living room, I caught the slump in his shoulders and the way he couldn't quite meet my eyes.

I knew he meant it. And I knew it was killing him.

* * *

Sebastian was right—I loved the job. It was better than I could have hoped. Over the next few years, I thrived on the intellectual stimulation. After nearly two decades of freelancing, it felt good to have colleagues and a steady paycheck.

Ryan said he was grateful for my new job, but he spiraled deeper into self-pity and depression. It hurt to see him so unhappy.

I knew his job situation was making everything worse. If he found something fulfilling, maybe it would pull him out of his rut. Maybe it would bring us closer again.

That's when I thought of Reiki.

Ryan had been good at energy work when we were dating. He had an intuitive way of moving energy, even if he hadn't practiced in years. With more training, he could be exceptional.

If he became so good he could charge $300 an hour, that wouldn't hurt either.

I started planting the idea gently. He didn't dismiss it outright, which felt like progress. Eventually, I convinced him to sign up for certification training.

I told myself it was about income. About confidence. About helping him reconnect with something meaningful.

But what I really wanted was the version of him I'd fallen for.

If he could find that again—if he could find himself again—maybe we could find our way back to each other.

Because as things stood, we weren't drifting—we were dissolving.

And I wasn't sure how long I could pretend otherwise.

* * *

"Minnie! That was amazing," Ryan said, as he burst through the front door a few months later, practically radiating positive energy. "What I learned at that tantra workshop years ago was just the tip of the iceberg. I learned so much more today, and it came so easily to me. The teacher said I was a natural conduit for channeling the energy."

A wave of relief—and satisfaction for pushing him to go—passed through me. "That's fantastic! I *knew* you'd be good at it."

"I'm… glad I went, so thanks for encouraging me." It was hard for him to say things like that, so I appreciated his acknowledgment all the more.

He was glowing, as if his body was still overflowing with all the energy he had channeled throughout the day. I loved seeing him like this.

Watching Ryan beam gave me a flicker of hope. Maybe the man I fell in love with wasn't entirely gone.

"So, wanna try it?"

I didn't even hesitate. "Of course."

We'd bought a massage table weeks earlier, back when he first signed up for the training, and now we were finally going to use it for something other than folding laundry. I climbed up onto it and closed my eyes.

I felt the warmth of his hands hovering just above me, but not quite touching. At first, it just felt like heat, but then I felt a change. I felt the subtle currents entering my body, almost like a caress, but without touching.

"Your body seems pretty calm, actually. But there's a lot going on up here." He hovered near my head. "Too much thinking."

That checked out. I wasn't holding any pain or stress in my body just then, but I had most definitely been thinking too much. I had worried all day about how his training was going, wondering if pushing him to go had been a good idea.

"All done," he said as he gently caressed my face. When was the last time he had done that? I couldn't even remember. This might be better for our relationship than I dared to hope.

I opened my eyes and sat up slowly. "Thank you," I said. "You're already good at this—and I know you'll only get better with practice."

He rubbed the back of his neck, proud and sheepish at the same time. "Thanks for pushing me to do this. I wasn't sure at first, but… yeah. You were right."

I grinned. "You say that like it's a rare occurrence."

He let out a laugh. "Oh, I told the whole class my wife made me come. Everyone else—seven women, by the way—was like, 'I felt called to healing work' or 'I want to deepen my spiritual practice,' and I was like, 'Uh… yeah, my wife signed me up.'"

I laughed, picturing it. "And it's good that I did."

"Yeah, yeah," he said, smirking. "You get full credit."

"Damn right I do. I'm writing it down." We both chuckled.

Then he grinned. "So… want to be my guinea pig for the next few weeks?"

I chuckled. "Lots of free Reiki? Yeah, I think I can make the sacrifice."

"Good. Because I'm officially a healer-in-training now, and you are going to be the calmest, most Zen wife in the neighborhood."

I smiled, watching him—really watching him. I felt something flicker back to life between us. Maybe—just maybe—this would be the thing that helped save our marriage.

* * *

Over the next month, Ryan poured himself into his Reiki training, and for the first time in years, he seemed truly engaged in something. He studied his materials and practiced on me regularly. I watched as the weight of his self-doubt slowly lifted, and as he started carrying himself with more confidence and ease. He wasn't walking around like a man who had failed anymore. He was someone with *purpose.*

Before the next training, he needed to gather twenty testimonials from at least ten different people, so we both started asking everyone we knew if they wanted a free session or two.

Quinn was the most amusing to me. He lay there for the full twenty minutes, eyes closed, utterly still—a rare thing for a ten-year-old—before giving the most honest review possible: "Eh? It was boring."

My sister tried to be supportive, but it wasn't her thing. She lay on the massage table, as stiff as a board, with her face frozen somewhere between polite skepticism and mild discomfort. When Ryan finished and asked how she felt, she gave him an awkward smile. "Um… good?"

Ryan took it in stride. Clearly, not everyone would be an ideal client.

Then there was Roxanne.

She worked with him at the grocery store where he'd been working part-time. She had arthritis in her hands, which made it difficult to do her job. But after just one session with Ryan, she said her pain disappeared—completely—for several days. When it returned, he worked on her again, and it vanished once more. They quickly fell into a rhythm. One or two sessions a week kept the pain at bay, but if she went too long without, it came creeping back.

For Ryan, it was tangible proof he was making a positive impact. He had always wanted to feel *useful*, and with her, he was.

She needed him, and he liked that.

* * *

I thought Ryan would grow his Reiki practice into his main occupation, but soon it became clear that wasn't his path. He enjoyed doing the sessions and was genuinely good at them, but something was holding him back from taking it further.

He never got to the point of having paid clients. He was still only doing free practice sessions, and the idea of asking for money made him visibly uncomfortable. Some part of him couldn't reconcile turning something so personal into a business.

He'd kept an eye out for other jobs the whole time, just in case something intriguing came along. When an aerospace sales position opened up, Ryan's whole demeanor changed.

"It's selling something clear," he said as he prepped for the interview. "Aircraft parts. Straightforward stuff. Detailed specs, predictable results. No guesswork."

He hesitated, then added, "With Reiki… I can't know if I'll have enough clients. I'm not even charging anyone yet. I can't build a life on maybe."

That was it. He needed the stability of a steady paycheck, the security of knowing there'd be work every day—and money coming in. Healing work was too unpredictable, too dependent on factors outside his control: clients, marketing, even his own comfort with asking for payment.

They offered him the job because of his Air Force background, and he accepted immediately. It was work he could feel confident about—something with clear parameters and predictable results.

Reiki had served its purpose. It had pulled him out of his rut and reminded him he could be good at something meaningful. He kept working with Roxanne because it truly helped her, and occasionally with me. Otherwise, Reiki faded into the background as he threw himself into his new job.

He whistled while he got ready for work and smiled when he came through the door at night. After so much uncertainty, after all the strain of the last several years, he had finally found something that fit.

Now that we were both fulfilled in our work, I let myself hope we would finally find our way back to each other.

Chapter 10. Reiki'd Over the Coals

Ryan's transformation at work was remarkable—he had energy and purpose in a way I hadn't seen in years. I should have been thrilled. And I was, at first. But as the months wore on, I couldn't shake the feeling that his happiness now existed separately from our marriage. He'd laugh on phone calls with colleagues, light up when his phone buzzed with certain messages, and carry himself with a confidence that felt both familiar and foreign.

But the space between us felt wider than ever. We were polite roommates, carefully avoiding the deeper conversations that might expose the emotional divide between us.

One evening, while we were in our bedroom folding laundry, Ryan broke our unspoken rule and suddenly asked, "Are you happy?"

His tone was casual, but I could tell he was anything but. What he really wanted to know was whether I was happy with him—with us.

I didn't answer right away, which probably gave him my honest answer. The truth was I wasn't happy, hadn't been for a long time, but I physically couldn't make the words come out.

With him finally happy at work, I'd believed our marriage would follow suit, but over the past few months he'd grown more distant, not less. But I kept telling myself that healing takes time. We'd spent years spiraling downward; it would take time to turn that around.

We'd had versions of this conversation before, and they'd never led anywhere. Eventually, the topic itself became radioactive. *Any* conversation about our relationship felt too uncomfortable to touch.

Now, folding underwear in our bedroom, I could feel that moment—his question—pressing in. A tiny opening. An invitation to be honest.

Honesty felt dangerous. What if he suggested changes I wasn't ready for? What if he agreed with me? What if he didn't?

So, I smiled weakly and said, "Yeah, I'm happy," and then changed the subject.

And he let me.

I didn't ask if he was happy. Something in his eyes suggested I wouldn't have liked the answer.

We talked about other, inconsequential things after that, but the weight of what we hadn't said filled the room.

* * *

I told myself this was the new normal. Ryan was content at work, Quinn was doing well at school, and I thrived in my job. We weren't passionate or deeply connected, but we were functional. There were good moments—weekend mornings making breakfast together and family movie nights. Maybe this was what marriage looked like after the honeymoon phase. Maybe I just needed to adjust my expectations.

Ryan seemed lighter. He had more energy, paid more attention to his appearance, and laughed more. Sometimes he took calls in another room, and I didn't ask about them—I assumed they were work-related. He was still new and wanted to be professional.

Roxanne still came by twice a week for Reiki. She and I would usually chat for a few minutes when she arrived, and over time it felt like we were becoming friends. I didn't have many local friends, so I welcomed the company.

After years of his depression and job struggles, Ryan's contentment felt like a gift. And I didn't want to question a gift.

* * *

"Mom! Big Scoop is finally open, and Dad said he would take me," Quinn announced as he ran through the kitchen at top speed on his way to his room for his shoes.

It was a beautiful spring day, and the local ice cream parlor had just reopened for the season. I was glad for them to have an outing together. I liked puttering around in the house by myself, and I didn't get to do that as often as I'd like.

Ryan followed shortly behind Quinn, smiling at Quinn's excitement. Then his demeanor changed, becoming uncharacteristically self-conscious. "So, ah," Ryan began, then cleared his throat. "Roxanne is meeting us there."

A small jolt went through me. "Oh?"

That was all I could manage to say—my brain hadn't caught up yet.

I knew all those Reiki sessions had turned into friendship. But this felt different.

This seemed a family outing. Just… with the wrong mother figure.

Oh, God. Was she *my replacement*?

The thought came out of nowhere—and I hated it.

I searched Ryan's face, trying to make sense of this.

More thoughts flooded in. *If I died, would he start dating her? Would she become Quinn's stepmother?* The idea made me feel a little sick.

I didn't know how to respond, and the silence stretched between us. He seemed to be waiting—almost begging me to ask a question he didn't know how to raise himself. And I just stood there, frozen in confusion.

"She's never been there since she's new to the area," he finally said to break the mounting tension. "So, ah, I thought it would be, you know, the friendly thing to do." He paused and smiled, and something about it made my stomach tighten. "I didn't think you'd want to go, since you've been avoiding sweets."

I nodded, unsure whether to be grateful he remembered or annoyed that he was taking someone else in my place.

It wasn't really about ice cream. They had planned to go without me, and that felt… deeply inappropriate.

And why was it always ice cream?

I didn't want the ice cream. I wanted to belong in my own family—not feel like the third wheel.

But instead of voicing any of that, I just said, "OK, I'll come too."

Ryan didn't argue, but he didn't smile either. He started tapping his phone as I headed to grab my shoes and coat. A moment later, Ryan called out from the other room. "Roxanne just texted. She can't make it after all."

A chill ran through me.

Why?

Was she avoiding me?

Why did Ryan seem so upset that she canceled? It was just a friendly outing to introduce her to Big Scoop, right? No big deal.

As the three of us headed to the car, I had a weird feeling I didn't understand. Then I realized it must be from considering my mortality. That would make anyone uneasy.

* * *

After the ice cream incident, I tried not to think about Roxanne becoming Quinn's stepmother if I died, but the discomfort lingered, like a low-grade headache I couldn't quite shake. I tried to ignore it and get on with life.

One Saturday morning, as I was contemplating how Ryan and I would ignore each other that day, he unexpectedly said, "I'm heading outside to plant your trees."

Finally. They'd been sitting out all week, their roots drying in the sun. I'd been worrying they'd die before he got around to it.

Just as I was about to feel a bit of relief—and maybe even a flicker of gratitude—a car pulled into the driveway.

That was odd. We weren't expecting anyone.

The door opened and out popped Roxanne.

Despite trying to put the ice cream incident behind me, I wasn't as comfortable with her coming around anymore.

"Ryan, is Roxanne here for Reiki?" I tried to keep the disappointment out of my voice. My trees would probably die after all.

"No, she's here to help with the trees." He paused, looking like he expected something from me. When all he got was a confused stare, he continued, "It's... uh, her way of paying me back for the Reiki stuff."

He couldn't charge money until he completed the final level, so this made sense.

Still, something didn't sit right, but I couldn't quite put my finger on it. I finally just said "Oh" and walked back into the kitchen to make a snack for Quinn. I told myself it wasn't a big deal.

But I kept glancing out the window.

The ground out there was rock-hard—solid clay and gravel, impossible to dig without real effort. I'd never been strong enough for that kind of thing. That was why I'd needed Ryan to do it.

I watched as he dug the holes, and she stood beside him, chatting and laughing. When he finished one, he'd place the tree in the hole, and she'd fill it in, tamp the dirt, and water it with the hose.

Geez. I could've done *that*—if he'd asked. If he'd wanted to do it with me.

I kept watching until I couldn't stand it anymore. There was too much ease between them. Too much smiling. Too much *not-me.*

I gave up and tried to read a book.

As I stared blankly at the pages, I couldn't stop thinking about it. About her. About them.

The feeling that she was here to replace me returned, and the worst part was—I didn't know what to do about it.

* * *

The weeks that followed brought a subtle shift in Ryan's routine. He seemed to have more evening plans—movies, errands, and other things that took him out of the house for a few hours at a time. I didn't think much of it at first. We'd been leading fairly separate lives for a while now, and honestly, I often enjoyed having the house to myself and Quinn.

However, I did start to notice that Ryan seemed different when he came home from these outings. Not bad different, but… energized in a way that our evenings together no longer made him. There was a lightness to his step, a distracted quality, as if part of his mind was still somewhere else.

One evening Ryan came home acting kind of jumpy, like someone who'd been doing something he wasn't supposed to.

Which didn't make sense.

He'd only gone to a movie, not a peep show.

Strange.

"So, what movie did you see this time?" I asked out of habit more than interest. He usually went to action films—loud, violent spectacles I had no desire to sit through—but I still asked. It was polite.

"*Cyrano,*" he said, looking me directly in the eye.

I felt a flicker of disappointment. It would have been fun to see that with him.

Cyrano was a romantic drama—soft, emotional, and poetic. The kind of movie *I* would want to see, not the kind he usually picked. Not the kind he would choose to watch alone.

"Why *that* movie?" I asked, genuinely confused.

He hesitated for just a moment. "Roxanne."

He paused, clearly waiting for me to react. Practically daring me to ask why. But I didn't say a word. I was speechless.

He wasn't alone.

"She got two tickets for her birthday," he continued, when I didn't take the bait. "Her husband didn't want to go, so she asked me. Said it was, you know, payback for the Reiki sessions."

Right. A fair exchange. Payment in favors, since he still couldn't charge money. Totally normal.

How many other movies had he gone to *alone*, except he hadn't actually been alone?

I couldn't stop picturing them sitting side by side in the dark, watching a love story unfold on the screen. Laughing at the same parts.

Maybe accidentally brushing arms, but *noticing*. Maybe sharing popcorn. Certainly feeling close.

I knew they were just friends, but it sounded like a date.

It *felt* like a date.

I didn't say anything. Just nodded and made a neutral sound.

Ryan looked… surprised. Maybe even a little disappointed—which made no sense, so I told myself I was misreading it.

When I clearly wasn't going to ask questions, he disappeared into his office.

I barely noticed him leaving the room. Inside, I was reeling.

Was I losing him?

Talking to Ryan about it felt impossible.

Not because I didn't care, but because I'd stopped believing that saying how I felt would change anything.

So, I did what I always did.

I swallowed it.

And went to bed with my heart full of questions.

* * *

I decided trying to be a better wife would be the best way to turn things around in our dysfunctional marriage.

I started small—expressing more gratitude for Ryan's efforts around the house and asking more questions about how work was going. He seemed to appreciate that.

I also tried to communicate physically. One day when he came into the bedroom while I was folding the laundry, I playfully lifted my shirt and flashed him. He used to like things like that and would smile and maybe caress me. I would always get a positive reaction. This time, though, he just stared at me and said nothing. The look he gave me said he wasn't interested in me or my body anymore, but that couldn't be it.

Shortly after that, I tried again when we went to the weekly farmer's market. While we were walking around, I slipped my hand into his, but he didn't react at all. It was like holding hands with a statue. I tried again—statue. I gave up. He used to enjoy holding hands, but now he seemed completely uninterested in any physical affection.

I started wondering if it was because we hadn't had sex in a while. Once that idea took root, I couldn't stop circling back to it.

I thought a lot about sex over the next few days. Not because I was horny—I barely remembered what that felt like—but because I felt guilty about how long it had been since the last time. Not only did I feel guilty about it, but I also felt guilty about how long it took me to feel guilty. It was pretty messed up.

Where had the sex-loving version of me gone? I missed her.

It didn't help that we were rarely even in bed at the same time anymore. Ryan's new job had him leaving before I woke up and coming to bed after I fell asleep.

* * *

Today, though, was a good day for sex. It was July 4th, so we didn't have to go to work. We had all day together, and a long session in bed was just what we needed.

After we were done, I gathered up my courage to talk about our relationship. It had been nearly six months since our last conversation like this, when he had asked if I was happy, and I had changed the subject. He'd caught me off guard, and I hadn't been ready for the conversation. This time, I was ready. He was usually more receptive to talking after sex, so this seemed like a good time to broach the subject.

"We need to talk," I said quietly. "About our relationship… and improving our sex life."

"Well, Minnie," he said, like he'd been waiting for this opening, "if we're going to work on our marriage… there's something I need to tell you." He paused briefly and gave me a piercing look. "I've been having an affair."

The air seemed to still around us, the cheerful chirping of birds outside our window a stark contrast to the silence that fell.

I didn't say anything right away. Even though my marriage hadn't been satisfying in a long time, it was still my foundation.

Having an affair…

As his words sunk in, I suddenly forgot all the times I'd wanted to leave him. I hadn't completely given up on us yet, and his betrayal was messing with my head big time.

I didn't know what to think, or even what to say.

"How many times?" was the only thing I could think to ask at that moment. If it had only been once or twice, maybe it wasn't so bad. I might understand that. Maybe.

"Don't you mean for how long?"

Whoa. This wasn't a one-time mistake but an ongoing betrayal, and he seemed so excited about it. And as if that wasn't bad enough, now he was making me beg for the details too.

"OK, for how long?" I obediently asked.

"Since December."

He started his new job in December. It all made sense now.

"Do you love her?" I didn't want to ask this question at all, but it was the most important one of all. I braced myself for his answer.

"Yeah, I do." Of course. His voice was soft at this confession, and he finally had the decency to look ashamed.

How dare he! He was taking away my hope, our better future. *Damn him!*

"Wait. Who are we even talking about?" I couldn't believe I hadn't asked this yet. "Do I know her?"

He paused as if surprised I needed to ask. "Roxanne."

Oh.

Her. Of course.

She really had replaced me.

A wave of nausea washed over me, and I thought I was going to be sick. I wanted to crawl under the covers and pretend this was all a bad dream.

"The movie last month… Why did you tell me you went with her?"

"Yeah, that," he said, rubbing the back of his neck. "I've been wanting to tell you for a while. I just… didn't know how to bring it up. I thought if you got suspicious, you'd ask. Then I could tell you. I even hoped you'd ask when I invited her to Big Scoop. Or when she helped with the trees."

His logic was so immature it left me reeling. He never knew how to bring it up? I guess the phrase "I have something I need to tell you" was not part of his vocabulary.

Like a fool, I'd trusted him completely, even though he had cheated before. *The best predictor of future performance is past behavior.*

"Why did you just have sex with me if you wanted to leave?" I couldn't believe this question was even relevant.

"Well, if you said no, I'd know we were done."

He'd been testing me. Lovely.

"But I didn't refuse. Now what?" I passed the test. What did that mean?

"I don't know. I really don't know…"

Great. Just… great.

My attention was grabbed by an odd feeling of ice running through my veins, a welcomed distraction from the pain that was threatening to overwhelm me. Was it adrenaline? Was my blood *actually* colder, or did it just feel that way? What emotion was I even feeling? I didn't know. Was I in shock? I didn't know. Probably.

What I *did* know was I felt like a colossal idiot. So incredibly naïve. I couldn't believe I hadn't realized what was happening right under my nose, even after he'd *tried* to make me suspicious.

It seemed like our conversation was over, so I stumbled into the bathroom for a much-needed shower. I didn't puke, but it was a near thing. The whole conversation felt surreal, like something from a nightmare.

Did that really just happen?

Chapter 11. He Left Me for That?

That afternoon, the sun was hot as I stood in the cemetery. The scent of freshly turned earth and decaying flowers was overwhelming. The grass was dry and crunchy beneath my sandals. It was quiet and peaceful.

I focused on these things to steady my mind—to calm my emotions.

"Hi Mom," I finally whispered. "I'm sorry I didn't visit sooner… I just couldn't bring myself to come…"

I gently set a chocolate chip cookie—Mom's favorite—on her gravestone. She had passed away two years earlier, and I needed her comfort and guidance now more than ever. I still missed her like crazy.

And I was glad she wasn't here to see this.

I sank down in front of the headstone and traced her engraved name. An agonizing knot twisted in my stomach. I still couldn't believe I was in this situation.

A spirit told me we'd have a baby, and against the odds, we did. Wasn't that proof Ryan and I were meant to be—until death do us part? How could something I'd been so sure was meant to be fall apart so completely?

Before I got married, Mom had tried to warn me about Ryan, about his past affairs. But I had been arrogant. I'd been convinced I knew better, that our relationship would be different. That he'd never stray.

"Mom, I was a fool." It was hard to say aloud. "I can't believe we let things get so bad that he thought an affair was a good idea. He should know better. He knows affairs ruin everything."

As my mind kept replaying the morning's conversation with him, a bug crawled on my leg. I pretended it was him and squashed it.

"Why did he do it? And how did I not notice?"

I felt like such an idiot for missing all the obvious signs. He was practically begging me to figure it out—and I still didn't.

And what kind of degenerate brings his lover into his home and suggests his wife befriend her?

"And get this—when I was trying to connect with Quinn's spirit before he was born, I pulled the Three of Swords, the divorce card, and I just shoved it back in the deck and told myself it meant nothing. On some level, I must have known." I wiped my nose with the back of my hand. Gross.

"And do you want to hear the most fucked-up part of all this? I felt closer to Ryan this morning than I have in years. Because we finally had a meaningful conversation. And part of me *liked* it, despite the topic."

I'd been starving for a real connection for so long that even a conversation about him falling in love with someone else was the most satisfying conversation we'd had in years. *What the hell?*

A breeze suddenly picked up, brushing my hair against my face like a caress. I closed my eyes and felt her there—just for a moment—as if she was trying to comfort me.

In my mind, I heard her. *Minnie, you're not an idiot. You're just human. Trusting and good-hearted. And maybe… maybe there's a deeper reason behind all of this—one you'll understand when the time is right.*

Maybe…

It seemed unlikely, though.

"I love you, Mom," I whispered as I stood to leave. "Thank you for always being there for me. Even when you're not."

And with that, I turned back toward the wreckage that was my life.

* * *

I barely slept that night, tossing and turning as I replayed not just every moment of Ryan's confession, but also everything Mom had said, in particular that maybe there was a deeper reason behind all of this.

When morning came, something had shifted inside me. I realized that if there was a deeper reason, then there must still be hope. My initial shock had been replaced with something I hadn't expected—determination.

I felt strangely calm. *I am going to save my marriage.*

We hadn't been able to fix it for over a decade, but suddenly I was convinced we could. This didn't strike me as delusional. No, I was a devoted wife, and I was going to do whatever it took.

In the cruel way that betrayal distorts reality, I had spent the night combing through our entire relationship—not for the ways he'd failed me, but for the ways I had failed him.

I told myself I'd been a bad wife. I had neglected him. I had pushed him away.

I completely forgot, however, about all the times I had reached for him and been ignored. I forgot about the years of loneliness. The conversations that went nowhere. The nights I cried in silence beside him in bed.

All of that was irrelevant now.

I would be whatever he needed. I would convince him to stay.

It didn't matter whether the marriage was worth saving. That wasn't the point anymore.

I hadn't been quite ready to let go. Now that it was slipping from my grasp, I clung to our marriage like my life depended on it.

I convinced myself that if I just held on tight enough, he would realize he loved me, not her. He would come back, and we would miraculously be happy.

So, when I walked into the kitchen and saw him sitting at the table, staring blankly at his bacon and eggs, I didn't rage. I didn't demand an explanation. I didn't ask why—I didn't have to. I knew I had driven him into her arms.

Instead, I sat across from him and said, "I forgive you… I want us to fix this."

He looked up with a blank expression. "You do?"

"Of course. I don't want our marriage to end like this." I sounded pathetic to myself, but I pressed on anyway. "I love you…"

"Okay."

Okay? Ouch.

He looked bored, dismissive even. "I don't know if it can be fixed."

Why isn't he cooperating?

"Can we at least try?"

He didn't answer right away. He just kept chewing as if he hadn't heard me, like we weren't talking about the possible death of our entire life together.

I watched him closely, searching his face for any sign—softness in the eyes, a twitch of the mouth, anything that meant I'd gotten through. Nothing.

Why doesn't he say something?

I offered a smile—small, tentative, like a peace offering. "Maybe we could go away for a weekend. Get a fresh start."

Still nothing. He just sat there and ate as I spiraled deeper into panic and clung even harder to the idea of saving my marriage.

Some small, stubborn part of me still wanted to believe it wasn't over yet, and it would do *anything* to keep him.

That's the thing about being betrayed—you don't automatically become wise and empowered.

Sometimes, you just become really committed to bad ideas.

* * *

Ryan was debating whether to stay or leave. He was torn. On the one hand, a marriage he had once been devoted to—and on the other, an exciting new lover.

He took responsibility seriously. I clung to that fact, telling myself it would be enough to make him stay. I knew he was still weighing things mentally, and I thought I could sway him. What I didn't realize was that while his mind was debating logistics, his heart had already packed its bags, moved out, and shacked up with another woman.

I begged him to give me another chance—to stay, to try one more time.

Humiliation didn't matter; I just wanted the opportunity. In the past, whenever one of us had tried to repair things, the other hadn't seen it—or hadn't been willing to meet the effort halfway.

This time felt different. We were finally talking. Really talking. Hours every evening.

It felt like the conversations Sebastian and I once had—deep, absorbing, electric. It felt like love to me. This time, however, they were happening in the shadow of another woman—and still I let myself believe they meant something.

* * *

A week into Ryan's internal debate, a week before Quinn's twelfth birthday, I suggested we take him to dinner and a movie—just the three of us, like we used to. "It might be good for Quinn to have some normal family time," I said, though we both knew I was really asking him to remember what he'd be giving up.

To my surprise, he agreed.

We went to Quinn's favorite restaurant, the one with the oversized burgers and games on the tables. Quinn was in his element, chattering about how fast he could ride the ATV, completely oblivious to the tension crackling between his parents.

Ryan seemed distracted, picking at his fries as Quinn told us he wanted to make a wooden sword. "So, Dad, when can we get started?"

"Sorry, buddy, what?"

"The sword! And can we paint it silver?"

Ryan glanced at me, and I saw something flicker across his face—maybe the realization that our "we" might not exist much longer. "Yeah, of course. We can make it Saturday."

At the movie theater, Quinn squeezed between us like he always did, sharing his popcorn and whispering commentary that made me laugh despite everything. During a funny scene, I caught Ryan watching Quinn instead of the screen. His expression was unreadable. When Quinn laughed at something ridiculous, throwing his head back the way he did when he was truly delighted, I saw Ryan's jaw tighten.

Halfway through the movie, Quinn leaned against Ryan's shoulder, the way he had since he was little. Ryan's hand automatically went to Quinn's hair, smoothing it down in that absent, protective gesture all parents know. For a moment, his face cracked open, and I saw the pain there.

On the drive home, Quinn fell asleep in the backseat. The car was heavy with unspoken words. Ryan kept glancing in the rearview mirror at our sleeping son.

"He's going to hate me," he said quietly.

I stared out the window. If he was looking for reassurance, I didn't have any left to give.

"Not if you stay…"

Ryan didn't respond. He just kept driving, his knuckles white on the steering wheel.

When we got home and helped Quinn inside, still half-asleep, it felt like we were still a real family. Maybe, just maybe, he could feel it too.

And then—

Ryan's phone buzzed. He glanced at it, and I saw his face change. Just slightly, but enough.

It was *her*.

He didn't even try to hide it.

Despite the lovely evening we'd shared, his heart was still with her.

* * *

A few nights later, I came home and found Ryan lying on the floor, tears in his eyes, his phone playing "I Won't Give Up on Us" like some melodramatic teenage breakup montage.

"That song," he whispered, voice hoarse, "it stabs me like a knife to the heart. I hate that I gave up on us. I never told you, but I used to have nightmares about cheating on you. I'd wake up in a panic, terrified it was real. Then I'd reach over, realize it was just a dream, and feel so relieved. And now…" He covered his face. "Now I've actually done it."

My chest tightened, but I made myself ask the thing I'd been avoiding. "How did it start? With her. The affair."

He exhaled slowly. "When I left the grocery store for the sales job, I started texting Roxanne now and then—just to check in and see how everyone was doing. It was innocent. At first. But then we started talking more. About work. About you and me. Our troubles."

He paused. "At the store, we couldn't really talk—too many people around. And during her Reiki sessions here… well, it didn't feel safe to go personal. You might overhear. But then, as we got closer, we started going out to lunch. I started meeting her at the park before work. But it was just as friends at first."

I nodded stiffly. "Affairs often start like that."

"I thought it was safe," he said, almost defensively. "I mean… I wasn't even attracted to her. Her head is kind of flat on top. I never thought I'd be interested in her romantically."

That was… an oddly specific detail.

"But the more we talked, the closer we got. Somewhere along the way… I don't even know when… I started seeing her differently. And then I couldn't stop."

It was so textbook it made me sick.

He looked at me, almost apologetically. "It's not because she's thinner or younger or prettier, if that's what you're thinking."

I hadn't been thinking that—until he said it. Now all I could picture was the gap between our ages, our bodies, our faces.

"She's eight years younger than me," I said flatly. "And thinner."

He didn't respond.

* * *

"I just don't care anymore," he said another night as we sat on opposite sides of the couch. "That's why I can talk to you now. I used to hold everything in because I was afraid you'd leave if I said something wrong."

I scoffed. "This is the cost of honesty? Total emotional detachment?"

"I'm not trying to hurt you," he murmured. "But yeah. I guess not being afraid makes it easier to tell the truth."

It was infuriating. I had spent years trying to get to this place with him—and now that I finally had it, it was only because he'd stopped caring. He wasn't afraid of hurting my feelings or making me angry. Or of me leaving him.

* * *

A few nights later, after another conversation that stretched past midnight, I looked at him across the kitchen table and took a shaky breath.

"I know I haven't been the best wife," I said. "I ignored your needs for a long time. I felt disconnected, and instead of trying to fix it, I just… withdrew."

He didn't say anything. Just kept listening, his brow slightly furrowed.

"I regret that so much," I went on. "If we had talked like this earlier in our marriage—if we had really opened up to each other—I think things could've been different. I know they could have."

He looked down at his hands, fidgeting slightly.

"But now…" I leaned forward, feeling the urgency rise in my chest. "Now that we're finally talking like this, I feel close to you again. I feel hopeful. If we keep this up, if we stay honest like this, I really believe we can make our marriage work."

He gave a small nod, but his eyes didn't meet mine.

"And honestly," I added softly, "I've always believed we were meant to be together. Because of Quinn. Because of how impossible it all was. The spirit. The tax refund. The guaifenesin. I believed it all meant something. That it wasn't random. That *we* weren't random."

He sighed and ran a hand through his hair. "Yeah… I mean, I don't know. Maybe."

His voice was quiet, but not reassuring.

I studied his face, waiting for something—anything—to confirm that he felt it too. That he believed there was still a future for us. But there was nothing there.

* * *

So, after hours and hours of raw honesty, after finally getting the depth of connection I'd desperately wanted for years, Ryan rented an apartment and moved out.

The weird thing was, after he moved out, we started spending even more time together. He came over every day—partly to see Quinn and the dog, but mostly because Roxanne hadn't moved in with him yet. And because his stuff was at his apartment, there was nothing for him to do but spend quality time with us.

We started acting more married than we had in years. Dinner. Dog walks. Shopping. Long talks. He kept doing "his" chores, like the yard work and handyman projects for me.

But it was all because he was biding his time.

This went on for a few confusing weeks. I would feel so close to Ryan while we went about acting married. Even listening to him talk about Roxanne helped me feel closer to him, because he was being so open and honest with me.

Part of me thought that, if I just waited—if I was just supportive enough—he would change his mind and come back to me. It was pathetic, and I knew it, but I couldn't stop myself.

* * *

Finally, the day came when everything shifted.

Roxanne was finally leaving her husband and moving in with Ryan. No more waiting. No more pretending. No more dinners and dog walks at my house. He wouldn't be coming back.

Today, she would start playing house with my husband.

I pictured them making dinner together, cuddling on the couch, heading into the bedroom. Images I did not need in my brain.

I stared at my phone, with my jaw tight. I didn't like it, but there was only one choice left.

I placed a call. To a divorce lawyer. I'd delayed divorce once before. I wasn't doing that again.

If my husband was going to be playing house across town with another woman, then it was time to make sure he officially became my *ex*-husband.

* * *

A few days later, I accidentally saw her.

My replacement.

She wasn't behind the deli counter where she usually worked, safely tucked away where I could easily avoid her. No, today she was out in the open, stocking shelves, moving slowly down the aisle without a care in the world—as if she wasn't the reason my marriage had imploded.

Attention, shoppers! Homewrecker in the deli aisle. Please stay clear for your own safety.

I didn't know why I still shopped here. It was my favorite grocery store, but there was always the danger of running into her. At least she hadn't seen me. I quickly ducked into the cookie aisle.

My pulse hammered in my ears. My vision started going dark around the edges, and tunnel vision started closing in. I gripped the cart handle so hard my knuckles went white, using it to steady myself as the floor seemed to tilt beneath my feet. My breathing turned shallow and rapid—this was *not* a good place for a panic attack.

It was the first time I had seen her since what I was now calling Disclosure Day—the day my world split into two: the time before I knew I had been betrayed and the time afterwards.

Now, with fresh post-betrayal eyes, I noticed details that had never registered before. Like how her head was weirdly flat on top—just like Ryan had said. He hadn't been attracted to her at first because of it.

I could see why. It was *so damn flat.* Maybe she wasn't even human, and that was just… how her people looked.

I swallowed hard, trying to push down the sting of him leaving me for that flat-headed maybe-alien. The fluorescent lights seemed too bright, making everything feel surreal and harsh. I could hear her voice now—something mundane about restocking—and it made my skin crawl.

This was the woman worth shattering our family over? God. The absolute *insult* of it.

Part of me knew it wasn't even about *her.* That part even knew I wasn't actually seeing her—I was projecting my pain onto her, reshaping her into something ugly in my mind. It hurt because I still wanted to believe *I* was special. Irreplaceable. But she was proof I wasn't.

The spirit hadn't mentioned another woman. I'd assumed we'd raise our child together. How could I have been so wrong about everything?

I took another slow, calming breath and forced myself to move on, to turn my cart in the opposite direction. But my hands were shaking so badly I could barely steer. I needed to get out of there as quickly as possible. I abandoned my cart right there in the cookie aisle and walked quickly toward the exit, weaving between other shoppers as if I was escaping a crime scene.

My breathing was still ragged when I reached my car. I sat there for a full five minutes before my hands stopped shaking enough to turn the key. One thought consumed my consciousness.

He left me for that?

But still, a small, pathetic part of me wished he'd come back.

Even after everything. Even now.

* * *

Over the next few weeks, I kept my distance from Ryan, only texting if there was a change in his plans with Quinn. Surprisingly, he kept coming over to mow the lawn—Quinn couldn't handle the whole yard yet, and I certainly didn't want to. He also kept bringing groceries, claiming he knew I hated shopping. I could tell he felt guilty about how everything had gone down—the affair, the lies, and not having the decency to leave me first. The constant helpfulness was his peace offering. I appreciated the help, but each time he came to the house, I disappeared into my bedroom anyway. I wasn't willing to play friendly soon-to-be-exes anymore.

But when it came time for Quinn's first overnight at the new love nest, I wanted to see my son off. I would emerge from my self-imposed exile and do my best to act like a mature adult.

When Ryan arrived, Quinn wasn't quite ready, so the two of us stood around awkwardly while our son gathered his things.

I wasn't exactly thrilled about Quinn spending time with *her*, but there wasn't much I could do about it. I *could*, however, probe Ryan for a little information about their new domestic bliss.

"So," I said, keeping my tone casual, "how's living with Roxanne working out?" It seemed like a safe place to start. And honestly, I *was* curious about the transition from an exciting, clandestine affair to folding laundry together. I wondered if it would be boring in comparison.

"Yeah, about that… She… won't leave her husband." He looked sheepish.

I snorted in surprise. "*What?* I thought she was living with you."

"She stayed two nights." He grimaced. "Then she went back to her husband. Said she needed more closure with him first. She keeps telling me she's moving back in with me, but she hasn't."

Well, well, well. Isn't that interesting.

"Wow," I said, trying to keep the highly entertained look off my face. "That… is a bummer," I said, resisting the urge to tack on a "S*erves you right.*"

"Yeah, and since then, it's been a total shit show. She keeps saying she's leaving him for good, but then she changes her mind. I don't know what the hell is going on anymore."

I nodded, pretending to be sympathetic, but deep down, I couldn't help but feel a little satisfied. Okay, *a lot* satisfied.

Ha ha. Take that.

Apparently, her species isn't big on follow-through.

Maybe I should've felt bad for him. I mean, I did. A little. He looked genuinely miserable, and I knew that kind of emotional whiplash was exhausting. I'd lived it firsthand, courtesy of him.

Another part of me—the petty, wounded part—was *pleased.* Because this was *exactly* what he deserved.

"You thought she was all in, huh?" I asked, still trying hard to look supportive, or at least neutral.

"She *said* she was. But now she keeps saying she's 'conflicted' and 'unsure' and…" He exhaled sharply. "I didn't sign up for this."

I almost laughed out loud. O*h, really?* I managed to suppress my glee. "So… let me get this straight. You left your wife for her, and now she can't decide if she actually wants to leave her husband for you?"

His jaw tensed. "Basically."

Oof. That had to sting.

There were so many not-nice things I could have said, but I just went with, "That sucks."

Because it did. But honestly? I was enjoying every minute of it.

Chapter 12. If the Ring Fits, Should You Wear It?

I *should* have just continued watching the "Ryan and Roxanne Rollercoaster Revue" from afar for the pure entertainment of it. I really should have. But things had changed for me.

Now that I knew she wasn't living with him, that she hadn't left her husband, something painfully pathetic had awakened in me. Every time he complained about her mixed signals, I analyzed his tone, searching for cracks in their foundation. I was secretly hoping their relationship would implode and he would come crawling back.

Oh, he wouldn't just come back. He would tell me what a huge mistake leaving had been, that he loved me and only me, that I was irreplaceable, and that he wanted to make our relationship amazing.

It was delusional, and I knew it. But knowing didn't stop the fantasy.

The problem was, I had so many different voices in my head, all wanting completely different things. One part of me wanted him back. Another wanted to cut him out forever. The vindictive part loved watching Roxanne torture him; the decent part wanted to be supportive. The practical part just wanted peaceful co-parenting.

I had so many competing voices inside me that I could've hosted my own inner podcast—"Conflicted AF, with your host: Also Me."

As entertaining as it was to obsess over the train wreck of Ryan's life, I was also trying to move on—or at least that's what I told myself. I bought new clothes and set up dating profiles, thinking that moving on meant I had to jump back into the dating pool. I talked to a few men online, but nobody measured up. None were ballroom dancers. But worst of all, they weren't Quinn's father—the man I'd built a whole spiritual narrative around.

The truth was, I wasn't really trying to move on at all. I was just rearranging the furniture while I waited for him to come home.

* * *

Quinn was handling his dad being gone pretty well, but I realized I had been neglecting him somewhat as I was dealing with the emotional upheaval. So, one Saturday morning, I decided he and I should try something we'd never done before—something completely unrelated to Ryan. I took him target shooting.

I would've never done this in Portland. But this was rural Ohio, where backyard targets get shot, deer get dressed in garages, and Amish kids casually bike past with hunting rifles every fall.

I had been concerned Quinn was a little young at twelve, but my friend Mike, a firearms instructor, gave us a strict safety briefing before teaching us how to stand, aim, and pull the trigger.

Quinn was all in. He was eager to learn and thrilled at the prospect of blowing things up—applied physics at its finest, in his opinion.

I thought shooting the guns was fun, but what really made it special was watching Quinn's joy every time he hit a target.

After the paper targets, we set up a pumpkin.

Man, that was fun to shoot. Quinn hit it first and put a hole all the way through it. My next shot sent a chunk flying, and soon, as we took turns, we shattered the pumpkin into a pulpy mess. His laughter was infectious.

If I imagined the pumpkin was someone's stupid bearded face—well, who would know that was why I enjoyed it so much?

We turned that pumpkin into mush. It felt good to watch something blow apart that wasn't my life.

Watching Quinn light up with every hit, I realized how badly I'd needed this—just the two of us. Maybe this was what rebuilding looked like.

"Mom, can you send the videos to Dad? He'll be so impressed!" *Yes, or he'd be jealous he didn't get to introduce Quinn to pulverizing pumpkins.*

"Sure, Sweetie." I really didn't want to. Part of me wanted to keep this to myself. I didn't want to bring Ryan into this memory in any way, but Quinn wanted to share it, and that outweighed my resentment. So, I sent the video.

For the first time in months, I went to bed that night feeling genuinely happy—as if maybe we could build a good life, just the two of us.

* * *

Early the next morning, my phone rang. It was Ryan.

I wasn't really in the mood to listen to him. But it could be important. He never called. He was a texting kind of guy. Something must be up. I stared at the screen, sighed, and then answered.

His voice was different—urgent, almost breathless. "I saw the video of Quinn."

Of course he did. I'd sent it to him. I could see from the app that he had viewed it.

"And…" I prompted.

He paused. Then, in a rush, he said, "I need to talk to you. I broke up with Roxanne."

That felt oddly beside the point. He was always bringing her up—and his news wasn't exactly a surprise. They'd already "broken up" at least twice in the past few weeks. It never lasted long. They would undoubtedly be back to sneaking around behind her husband's back in a day or two.

"Oh. Do you want to talk about it?" I asked, already gearing up for another juicy Roxanne postmortem.

"No. Not this time." His voice softened. "It's done with Roxanne. Really done. I realized I miss you. A lot. I miss our family. Seeing you and Quinn out without me… watching someone else teach him things that should've been me… I don't want to lose that. I want us back."

What had he thought would happen to our family if he left? He had to realize we would move on, eventually. But now that it was happening, even in a small way, he didn't like it.

The part of me that wanted him to come back was doing a happy dance in my mind—confetti, fireworks, the whole shebang—while another part stood trembling in the corner, whispering, "Don't do this again." But of course, the happy part was louder. Isn't it always?

I figured I'd have to consider it—or risk being haunted for the rest of my life by the world's most annoying ghost: *What If.*

I'd only consider it if he could keep showing up the way he had been since Disclosure Day, though—with honesty and presence. Anything less, and I knew I wouldn't survive another round.

"Okay," I said slowly. "Let's discuss it after work." The war going on in my head was making me tired, and this seemed an in-person kind of discussion, anyway.

"Yeah, okay," he said. "I'd like that."

I hung up the phone and just sat there, staring into space.

Could this be it? Could this be how we finally saved our marriage? By having to go so low? The betrayal. Him moving out. Me starting to move on. Was this the turning point where we finally got it right?

Or was I just deluding myself—again?

I would find out soon enough.

* * *

When he came over after work, Ryan still wanted to see if we could reconcile. I had kind of thought he'd change his mind. It had been a whole eight hours—plenty of time for my replacement to reclaim him. But no. Not yet anyway.

"I want to move back home," he said quietly. "I don't want to live in that apartment anymore. It reminds me of her. Of everything I messed up."

I stared at him. He looked so earnest. So vulnerable.

It tugged at my heart.

It was probably a bad idea, but I was willing to consider it—but there would be conditions. "If you want to move back in, you have to cut off *all* contact with Roxanne. No calls, no texts, no 'just checking in to see how she's doing.' If we're going to try this again, she can't be part of your life *at all*."

He nodded immediately. "I know. I already told her it's over for good. And you can read my messages. Anytime you want. I won't hide anything from you."

I wanted to believe him. He wasn't exactly trustworthy, but if I could verify his promises—if I could watch him keep them—then maybe, just maybe, we had a chance.

The truth was, I missed him. I missed being a family.

"Yes, okay. You can move back in. On a trial basis. And I'll be checking your messages."

He looked so happy and relieved. "Yeah, of course. So… can I start moving my stuff back in tonight?"

Whoa!

"Tonight?" I mean, I guessed that made sense, but I was still getting used to the idea. I'd thought I'd have a few days to adjust.

"Yeah. I just… I don't wanna stay there anymore. Not even one more night. Everything in that place feels wrong."

I hesitated. It was so sudden.

But I also knew what he meant. That apartment was a shrine to his mistakes. If we were going to try again, maybe we needed to reclaim the life we'd had. Right now, before doubt took over. Before *she* got her hooks into him again.

I took another calming breath. "Okay. Tonight."

Relief flooded his face. "I swear I'll make this right."

We stood up, and just like that, we were in motion again—grabbing our keys and heading out the door together to collect the scattered remnants of his other life. *His preferred life*, a part of me whispered.

But I didn't listen. Maybe that part was wrong.

* * *

The next day, Ryan came over after work and walked in without knocking because he was *living with me* again. It felt weird. And it was weird that it felt weird because I hadn't really become accustomed to him being gone yet.

As we sat at the dinner table, I noticed his hands. Specifically, the wedding ring on his left hand.

I had noticed it before, in passing, but it hadn't fully registered until now—he had been wearing it the whole time.

"Did you forget you're still wearing your ring?" That seemed more plausible than him choosing to still wear it.

He looked down at his hand. "Yeah, about that. I guess I had never completely given up on us."

Well, that was a surprise. It could also explain why Roxanne was having trouble leaving her husband for him.

It was confusing. I had spent months feeling abandoned. Discarded. I'd watched him obsess over another woman while I tried—and failed—to keep my dignity intact.

Nonetheless, here he was, telling me he had still been holding on—at least symbolically.

I glanced down at my own bare hand.

I hadn't worn my wedding ring in years. At first, it had been because of pregnancy weight. I hadn't wanted to resize it, only to lose weight and need to resize it again. Then after a while, it was because our relationship was so often on the brink, so what would be the point?

Ryan took my hand and rubbed his thumb over my finger where my ring used to be. "I never said anything, but… it always bothered me you didn't wear yours."

I looked up from our hands, surprised. "It did?"

"Yeah. It felt like maybe I was the only one still holding on."

That made me feel like a heel. I'd never let myself think about how it would make him feel. What a mess we were.

"I hate how things ended up, and I know I screwed up. But I want us to really try this time. *Really* try." He paused. "Would you have it resized? I… I'd really like to see you wear it again."

The lump in my throat rose so quickly I couldn't speak.

I hadn't expected this. I had been prepared for cautious rebuilding. Essentially dating again, even though he had moved back in. But this?

It felt like real commitment—to me, to us. It was surprisingly touching.

I blinked back tears and nodded. "Okay." I needed to give it my all.

Wait. What was I agreeing to? He had left me for another woman and was possibly only considering me again because she wouldn't commit to him.

But still… I had to take the chance. It was madness—a hopeful kind of madness.

I imagined him slipping the ring back onto my finger, like a recommitment ceremony. I could just see it—he would look deeply into my eyes, tell me how he'd lost his way, but he had found his way back. He would tell me how much he loved me and how he couldn't live without me. He would *choose me* and slide the ring onto my finger. We would shed a few happy tears.

This was definitely the start of something new.

Yes, this time, we'd get it right.

* * *

The next evening, we sat in his car, waiting for our carry-out order to be ready. We were chatting about our day, but something felt off. There was a little more tension between us than there had been the day before.

I wanted to believe everything was fine, that he hadn't been in touch with Roxanne, but I couldn't trust him anymore. I needed proof.

"Hey, since you offered, let me see your messages." Time to see if he'd been sincere about that.

The sudden alarm on his face gave me my answer. He quickly scrolled through his messages, then slipped his phone into his pocket.

He had promised he wouldn't be in touch with her. He had *promised.* And he had *betrayed me*. Again.

Why had I agreed to take him back? *Why, why, why?* Because hope still made me really stupid, that's why.

I stared out the windshield, jaw locked, willing myself to stay calm. I didn't trust myself to speak. Not at first. Not without screaming.

Finally, I inhaled slowly and said, with deliberate quiet, "You're not sleeping in my bed tonight." I should have said something more like, "Take me home, then get the hell out of my life." I was so hurt, though, I just shut down and could only put up the weakest barrier.

He turned to look at me, confused. Hurt, maybe. What the hell was there for him to be confused or hurt about? It was blatantly obvious what was wrong.

I didn't know yet if I wanted him to sleep in my guest room or go back to his apartment. I didn't want to decide anything immediately, but I at least knew I didn't want him in my bed.

He opened his mouth as if he was going to say something, but I turned my back to him and looked out the side window.

I needed some time and space to process this latest indignity, but I was stuck in his car, marinating in this awful knowledge, pretending I hadn't just seen the truth on his lying, cheating face.

* * *

The next morning, I stood at the counter of the jewelry store, alone.

My ring wasn't ready yet—but that was the point. I wanted to pick it up before wasting money on resizing it.

After the previous night, after the way Ryan looked at me when I asked to see his phone, I didn't need to wait until the resizing was done.

I already had my answer.

He would *never* be over her, and I would never wear that ring again.

The jeweler set the small velvet box on the glass counter. My ring nestled inside looked exactly the same—shiny, beautiful.

Un-resized.

"We haven't had a chance to resize it yet," he said gently. "Would you like to leave it until tomorrow?"

I shook my head in embarrassment. "Change of plans. I don't need it resized after all." *Oh, God. What must he be thinking? Am I the lamest customer ever?*

He hesitated as if he might say something—then saw my face and thought better of it. He nodded once and stepped away in silence.

I grabbed the box and snapped it shut. I didn't want to see it anymore. Maybe I should sell it to the jeweler. But that was a decision for another day.

For now, I would just take it home and store it next to the rings from Sebastian. I never meant to collect wedding rings. Or ex-husbands.

The drive home felt endless. I kept glancing at the ring box, the tiny coffin for my hopes. I knew Ryan would ask about it the moment he walked through the door, and I was trying to decide exactly how to say, "I'm not wearing it while you're still in touch with your fuck buddy."

* * *

When Ryan came home from work that evening, I was in the kitchen pretending to scroll through my phone, but I was really just getting ready to tell him to pack his bags and leave.

"I'm sorry," he said before I could say anything. "About last night. She contacted me yesterday. I responded. I couldn't help it. I felt ashamed for breaking my promise to you—but I'm really trying to let go of her. I just—it's going to take some time. I'm not there yet. But I *am* trying." He looked so remorseful, so earnest.

It hit me right in the heart.

Oh, good God. How much emotional whiplash could I stand?

He held out his phone. "Here. Look. Nothing from today. No calls, no messages."

It was true—but he didn't scroll back to yesterday's messages. Maybe it didn't matter. He was trying. He succeeded today. I could give him that.

Part of me wanted to believe him.

"Please give me another chance. I'll show you my messages every day. I promise. Please, let's drop your ring off again."

I hesitated. And then, like a pathetic fool, I simply nodded and off we went to the jewelry store, again.

* * *

The next evening, I was rinsing dishes in the sink, eagerly awaiting Ryan's arrival. He had texted at lunchtime to let me know he had picked up my ring.

When I heard him open the door, I dried my hands. This was it! We were going to grab hold of our relationship and not let go. All symbolized in a band of gold.

He walked into the kitchen with his head down and his shoulders hunched. That was odd. I wondered what happened at work to make him look so downtrodden.

Just as I was about to ask, he tossed the ring box onto the counter without looking at me—then walked to the guest room and shut the door.

I was so shocked I just stood there.

What the hell was going on?

Where was our sweet moment? *He* was the one who suggested this.

Had he changed his mind? Had he contacted Roxanne again? I was being naïve—*again.* Of course he had.

I picked up the box and opened it. I stared at the ring for a long time.

He wasn't here with me, but he still gave it to me. That had to mean something, didn't it?

I felt ridiculous. Stupid.

If the ring fits, should you wear it? The answer really should have been *"Hell, no!"* But I slid the ring onto my finger anyway—alone.

It was so lame I could hardly stand myself.

I studied my hand, expecting… something. I thought it would make me feel closer to him to wear this ring again. But all I felt was foolish. So damn foolish. And full of regret.

The evening dragged on forever. He never came out of the guest room. He was probably texting *her*—again.

By the time I climbed into bed, I felt more alone than I had when he had first moved out. *What the hell?* I stared at the ceiling. The gold shackle on my left ring finger felt very heavy. I debated taking it off, but I decided to wait until the next day.

Lying there in the dark, I couldn't help but wonder, *How many times am I doomed to repeat this cycle of hope and disappointment?*

* * *

The next evening, when Ryan came home from work, I braced myself. I was surprised he hadn't moved out that morning—which meant this wasn't over yet.

From down the hall, the faint thump of Quinn's music bled through his door. Lucky kid—he got to tune out the real noise.

As we made dinner, Ryan avoided eye contact. I didn't want to ask what was going on. I didn't need to. I already knew. I asked anyway—to get it over with.

"Did you contact Roxanne?"

The flicker of guilt was instant. His shoulders dropped a bit. *Yep.*

"She contacted me," he said quietly. "Said she missed me… that her life wasn't worth living without me. She sounded… like she might… take that literally. I couldn't ignore that." He looked at me, pleading for understanding.

There'd be no understanding coming from me. If she really did "take it literally," it seemed to me that was something *her* husband—not mine—should deal with.

"I couldn't help it," he went on, trying to make me understand. "I didn't know what else to do. She said she needed me, and… I just went. I don't even know what the hell I'm doing anymore. It's so complicated."

He said it like it was confusion, not betrayal.

His face twisted between guilt and something worse: affection. But the affection was not for me.

"No," I said, my voice surprisingly calm. "It's not complicated at all. It's actually very simple."

He looked surprised. Maybe confused.

"Gather up your clothes," I said. "And get the hell out of my house."

He flinched, as if I'd slapped him. His lips parted, soundless for a second.

"Wait…"

I didn't wait.

I yanked the ring off, held it up for a second, then tossed it onto the table. It clinked once and went still.

Then I went to my bedroom and locked the door behind me.

I felt like such an idiot for even considering reconciliation, for hoping, for letting him in.

I was glad Quinn was in his room playing loud music, unaware of what was happening between us.

A few minutes later, I heard the sound of drawers opening. Then the front door opened and shut.

Ryan was gone—again.

I cried myself to sleep.

* * *

Our court date was two weeks later. We'd have canceled it if our ill-fated reconciliation had worked. But no. So the divorce remained the one stable commitment in the situation.

I was still pissed at him about going back to her. It was hard to keep track, but I think they had gotten back together, broken up, and gotten back together again since I kicked him out. At that point, I wasn't even sure if they were together or broken up.

Even with all that, part of me *still* wanted him to call off the hearing. That desperate, insane part wanted Ryan to beg me to take him back, especially since things still weren't going well with Roxanne.

That part wanted him to swoop in for a dramatic, romantic moment where we saved our marriage from the jaws of death, proving I was more worthy and desirable than her. The other parts of me wanted that desperate, insane part to shrivel up and die a painful death—as soon as possible.

Life isn't a movie, so he didn't stop the proceedings.

Instead, just four months after Disclosure Day, it was time to Zoom in for our court hearing. My heart had not caught up with the rapid pace of everything. Four short months was not enough time to process all the conflicting emotions.

In a moment of weakness, I had asked Ryan to come over for the hearing. It was bad enough we were going through with it. At least I wouldn't have to be alone for it.

That also gave him one last chance to call off the hearing. But he didn't. *Jerk.*

So, now we were sitting side by side at my kitchen table, with my laptop open, our bodies close but not touching. No longer *together*.

The judge moved through the process quickly, efficiently—just another case, just another couple untangling their lives. The moment came and went without fanfare. No last-minute confessions. No grand gestures. Just a legal proceeding, over in a few minutes, reducing years of hope and struggle to an entry in a court record.

When it was over, we sat there for a few moments in silence. What do you say after that?

I stared at the laptop screen, watching the judge's face disappear as he ended the call. Just like that: fourteen years of marriage, dissolved in a few minutes of legal formalities. I kept waiting to feel something—anger, relief, sadness, anything—but there was just... nothing.

It was like watching someone else's life through thick glass. I could see what was happening, but I couldn't quite connect to it. This couldn't be real. This couldn't be my life.

I felt like a zombie—present but not really there, going through the motions of being human while something essential had been switched off inside me.

The laptop fan hummed quietly. Outside, I could hear our dog barking. No, *my* dog now. A car went by, the sound drifting through the window like something from another world. Normal life, continuing around us while ours officially ended.

I really should have thought through how awkward this moment would be when I invited him over.

Ryan looked sad and guilty. I don't know how I looked. Sad, for sure. Disappointed? Resigned? Angry? Conflicted? Probably some of all that.

We reached for each other at the same time. We shared a bittersweet hug. Maybe our last one ever. I felt his strong arms around me and knew things would never be the same. He wasn't mine anymore. He belonged to someone who still hadn't chosen him.

I wanted to say something—I don't know what, but *something*—but before I could, he pulled away. The moment was lost.

He picked up his phone and keys and then paused at the door. "So… I guess that's it, then." His voice caught just a little before he turned and walked out.

Fuck.

I was divorced.

Again.

It wasn't supposed to end like this.

No sense of closure. Just the click of the door, and he was gone.

Chapter 13. Fuck Being Nice

The divorce *should* have been the end of it. I *should* have been focusing on moving on—on healing and rediscovering myself. I *should* have been burning sage in every room to rid the place of bad ex-husband juju.

At first, it felt like I was moving on. I did more redecorating. I removed every photo of Ryan from the walls. I put up artwork he didn't like. I replaced all my bedding because—*eww.*

I even went to a therapist, but he wasn't very helpful. He mainly told me I should never talk to Ryan about anything other than logistics about our son. That I shouldn't even let him come to the door when he picks Quinn up. That seemed extreme and unnecessary. I wanted us to at least be amicable co-parents for Quinn's sake. Shutting Ryan out like that didn't seem amicable.

I thought I'd come to terms with being apart. Part of me even thought I was free. Oh, how wrong that part was.

Letting go of ex-husbands wasn't one of my signature strengths—even if he lied, cheated, and used me when he was lonely. Apparently, I hadn't dropped low enough yet. I hadn't become angry enough yet.

After our divorce, Ryan and I barely talked for a few weeks, but then we started chatting a bit again. I found out Roxanne still hadn't moved in with him, and it was wearing on him. He seemed to have thought she'd finally move in with him now that he was divorced. Nope, that didn't fix her commitment issues.

She would promise to move in once or twice a week, but she'd change her mind—every time. I don't think she was stringing Ryan along on purpose, but the end result was the same, and he was getting increasingly frustrated.

I was back to finding the whole thing entertaining, but I kept that to myself and tried to be supportive—at least on the surface. That way, I could keep getting the juicy details. Even though I thought I was trying to live my own life, I was actually highly invested in Ryan's suffering. It made me feel better about our situation.

It wasn't that I *wanted* him to suffer. Okay, actually I did. Just not *too* much—he was still the father of my child, after all. But there was a certain deliciousness in watching him get whipped back and forth to the point of a near breakdown.

Every time he sighed over another broken promise or whined about Roxanne's hot-and-cold routine, I nodded sympathetically while privately savoring it like a piece of rich chocolate. Was it healthy? Probably not. Was it satisfying? Most definitely.

He'd left me for her. He had blown up our life for her. So, if he was now stuck navigating her emotional boomerangs and commitment-phobia… Well, it was the most entertaining soap opera ever.

I kept listening, and he kept opening up more. He didn't have anyone else to turn to for emotional support, and I felt like a good person for letting him.

He also started spending more time with me when he came to my house again, first just a few minutes, but it quickly escalated to over an hour of deep, heartfelt conversations—practically every day.

Over the weeks our conversations started slowly shifting. Oh, he'd still tell me all the latest about her, but he was getting friendlier with me. Flirtatious even.

I knew I should put a stop to it, but I didn't. I flirted back. I knew it was a bad idea, a *terrible* idea. The worst possible idea.

But it was sort of fun. Flirting with your ex is a strange drug—intoxicating and confusing, in equal measure.

* * *

Maybe he thought it was fun, too. Or maybe he was just lonely. Maybe that's why one evening, about six weeks after our divorce, he suggested we go to a movie together.

With all the recent flirting, I needed to be clear about what he was asking.

"Like… a date?" Did I want it to be? Would he be cheating on her with me if it was? That would be ironic.

I had wanted him back previously. Did I still? I wasn't sure. I wasn't a woman desperately trying to save her marriage anymore. If we went down this road now, I'd just be a lame divorcée who couldn't let go.

His face turned slightly pink. "Maybe. I don't know. I just… I need a night out. I know… Let's take Quinn. It can be a family outing."

We weren't a family anymore—not in the traditional married-couple-with-a-kid sense—so it wouldn't really be a family outing.

It probably wasn't a date. He was likely just lonely and wanting some company. And so was I.

I was confused about his intentions—and mine—but, unwisely, I agreed to the outing.

At the theater, Ryan positioned himself between Quinn and me. If this was just a way for us both to spend time with Quinn, it seemed like he should have been between his divorced parents, so we could both whisper to him during the movie.

Did the seating arrangement mean anything? Was I making up intentions that weren't there?

I tried to relax and just enjoy the movie, but halfway through, it became impossible because Ryan suddenly put his hand on my leg!

I froze, not knowing quite what to do. Push it away? Put my hand on his? Pretend it wasn't there? What was he up to?

The surround sound boomed, laughter rippled through the darkened theater, and I had no idea what was happening onscreen anymore.

He eventually removed his hand, and I wasn't sure if I was happy about that.

Before I decided, he put his hand on my leg again!

We were acting like two awkward teenagers who didn't know if touching at the movies was okay. It really shouldn't be okay for us. We were divorced. His heart belonged completely to someone else, even if she treated commitment to Ryan like a contagious disease.

The gesture left me feeling unsettled and unsure of his intentions, and uncertain about what I wanted. Was he just messing with me? Did he want to reconcile? Have a fling?

Did I want to risk getting burned again? Did I want to be anywhere near his rollercoaster of a life? The answer should have been a clear no. A strong *no fucking way.*

But somehow, it wasn't clear at all.

* * *

The next morning, I woke up confused, but a tiny bit hopeful. He'd planted the idea—maybe unintentionally—but I couldn't stop thinking about it. Maybe he had realized he still loved me and wanted to come back. Maybe we could rebuild something better than ever out of the ashes of our past.

That desperate, insane part of me that wanted him back had not yet shriveled up and died. It had woken up, and it was *thrilled.* And it was suddenly in charge again.

I needed to know what Ryan was thinking. I whipped out my phone and texted him. "Were you just messing with me yesterday when you put your hand on my leg?"

He texted back immediately. "No, I wasn't messing with you. I miss you."

Translation: Roxanne had been yanking his chain too much, and he wanted to feel better about himself again. And his easiest way to do that was to get validation from me.

I missed him, too. Or more accurately, I missed having *someone* as a partner. I hadn't become comfortable with being on my own yet, and that made me vulnerable.

That exchange left me more confused than ever. Before I could figure out what any of it meant, Christmas was bearing down on me—my first one as a divorced woman.

The holidays are a terrible time to be lonely.

I was weak.

We had family traditions that I thought I'd never get to do again. I had been sad about that. It just wasn't the same without him. But now he was dangling the possibility of togetherness in front of me. How could I say no?

And so, even though I figured it would only last for a few days at best and I would end up getting burned, I invited him to come over for Christmas Eve.

* * *

After making cookies for Santa and gorging on the traditional Christmas Eve pizza, we were ready to watch *The Grinch*. Ryan patted the seat next to him as he wiggled his eyebrows suggestively.

I hesitated ever so briefly, but that desperate, insane part of me was still in charge, so I curled up beside him. I told myself Ryan was really interested in me—not just biding his time while Roxanne figured out her shit. Deep down I didn't believe it, but it was soothing to pretend. His arm around my shoulders felt pleasantly familiar.

Quinn plopped down in the recliner, with a cat and a bowl of popcorn balanced on his lap.

It all felt so normal, so right.

After the movie, Quinn went to bed, and Ryan and I ate the cookies we had left out for Santa and set out the presents. It was so sweet, so comforting.

I wasn't ready for the evening to end. I didn't want to be alone. I wanted to hold on to this feeling that everything was back to normal a bit longer—at least into Christmas morning.

"Will you spend the night?" I knew I sounded pathetic, but I tried to ignore that.

He hesitated, emotions flickering across his face. "Yeah… okay. Just tonight, though. I can't promise more than that."

I knew he was lonely too. And I knew we were using each other. To get through the holiday, though, I was okay with that.

* * *

In the morning, when it was Ryan's turn to open his only present, I handed him a small wrapped box.

He peeled back the layers and held up a black lump. "Is this… coal?"

"Charcoal soap," I said. "So technically yes, but also you're welcome."

He laughed. "Wow. Message received."

"Hey, I didn't know you'd be here. You're lucky you got anything."

We opened the rest of the gifts, ate more cookies, and made it through the morning without any weird tension. Quinn was thrilled to have both parents there. Ryan was present, the way I had always wanted him to be all those frustrating years. I didn't think it would last. Still, I was quietly grateful for one more holiday together.

* * *

The Christmas morning glow didn't last long. Within days, we were back to our confusing dance of mixed signals and false hope.

Over the next few weeks, Ryan alternated between sending me flirty text messages and messages about his saga with Roxanne. The possibility of future reconciliation was on the table again, but we were in a wait-and-see pattern. Could he let go of Roxanne? (Of course not.) Would I put up with his shit again? (Apparently so.)

I responded in kind to the flirty ones and supportively to the ones about my replacement. Part of me seemed to think that, if I was really supportive, he would realize I was the better choice and come back. Another part of me knew I was being a damned fool. Part of me thought the flirting was fun. Part of me was simply delighted to see Roxanne rip him apart (while ignoring the fact that he was doing the same to me).

Since part of me enjoyed the flirting so much, I fully participated in the escalation from flirtatious texting to full-out sexting. That was new for us, and it was really fun.

I enjoyed it perhaps a little *too much*. I enjoyed it so much that, one morning, I needed to disappear into my bedroom for a bit. Then I texted and told him about it.

He didn't respond to that, but I assumed he was just busy.

He was planning to come over after work, and I couldn't wait to see him. Maybe we'd get a little physical. I was a bit tingly in anticipation.

When he arrived, he was acting distant and aloof.

Damn it.

The tingles disappeared immediately. I was pretty sure I knew what had happened.

Roxanne.

Roxanne happened. Roxanne would *always* happen.

She must have changed her mind yet again, or at least said something encouraging to him to get his hopes up again.

Why did he have to get *my* hopes up? Why did I allow it? *Why, why, why?*

Deep down, I had known this would happen—it was just a matter of when, but part of me still hoped I was wrong, that this time would be different.

I wanted confirmation, but I wasn't going to make it easy for him. In fact, I was going to make it really awkward for him.

"So… I really enjoyed the sexting this morning," I purred. "Maybe we could go… cuddle… in my bedroom."

I'd have been shocked if he agreed. Shocked and freaked out, actually, because I really didn't want to even be in the same room with him with the mood I was in, let alone "cuddle." *Ugh.*

"Yeah, about that… Um… Sorry. I didn't mean to lead you on. But Roxanne changed her mind. She's moving in tomorrow."

I'd be willing to bet my house and both of my legs she wouldn't really move in with him the next day.

But *he* believed her, of course.

So, just like that, he was completely hers again. Unbelievable. *I can't fucking believe I was letting him in again.*

"So… why were you sexting me this morning when clearly you were texting Roxanne, too?"

"Oh, well… I was trying to help you stay interested in sex. I didn't mean for you to be thinking about me in particular."

Oh. My. Freaking. God.

It just gets more humiliating by the second. I thought we were having a meaningful connection this morning. *Not even close.*

I didn't recognize myself anymore—and I hated who I'd let myself become.

Something inside of me snapped.

I didn't want to know anything else about it. In fact, I didn't want to know anything else about him for the rest of his godforsaken life.

So fucking done with him.

"Get the fuck out!" I couldn't believe I'd thought he would *ever* change his mind. He would *never* get over her. He didn't even *want* to. He just wanted me as a backup plan when he was lonely. Well, *fuck that. I'm nobody's unwanted consolation prize.*

"But…"

"Out!"

The second the door clicked shut behind him, I grabbed our wedding album and tore it to shreds, page by page, until there was nothing left but scraps.

Then I yanked our wedding portrait—the one I had just rehung that morning—out of its frame and burned it on the driveway. Burning something had never felt so satisfying.

Oh my God! The messages! I grabbed my phone. I deleted our entire texting history from both of our accounts. Every message. Every image. Every humiliating word. I would rather *die* than let him read them again. I couldn't believe I told him about masturbating this morning. He was probably texting *her* while I was screaming his name, alone, in my bedroom. Unbelievable. Just fucking unbelievable.

I will never let myself behave so pathetically again. Never.

After I finished destroying every trace of our marriage, I still had one more act of reclamation left. I went to the furniture website where I'd been debating between two couches all week. One was a plain brown sectional—boring and practical. Ryan's style. The other was a bold, curvy red velvet masterpiece that I'd fallen in love with the moment I saw it.

When I'd shown both options to Ryan, he had said, "If we end up together again, I could imagine the brown one feeling like *our* couch, in *our* living room, in *our* house someday. But if you buy the red one… that'll always be *your* couch. In *your* house."

Damn straight, it's all mine.

No more beige compromises. No more dimming my colors to make someone else comfortable.

Let him have his beige life with her. I would have curves, color, and pleasure in mine.

I ordered my gorgeous red velvet couch.

* * *

For the next week, I was so furious with Ryan I could barely function. I couldn't work. I couldn't focus on anything except what a selfish, immature jerk he was. I did my best to stay composed in front of Quinn, but, when he was at school, I screamed. I cried. I raged. I paced around the house like a caged tiger, replaying every lie, and every betrayal.

I had never been so mad in my life. What I'd felt before was nothing compared to the all-consuming rage I felt now.

And it just lasted and lasted. I didn't think I'd ever feel anything but fury ever again.

During my weekly call with my friend with whom I studied a therapeutic approach called "parts work," I launched into another rant about what an absolute asshole Ryan was. She listened for a while, then gently stopped me. "Say it in 'parts language.' *You* are not angry. *Part of you* is angry."

I was annoyed she had cut off my rant, but this was the point of our calls—to help each other reframe our thinking in terms of our "internal parts." So, I humored her.

"Fine. *Part* of me is SO FUCKING ANGRY…"

That one sentence shifted everything.

As soon as I said it, I "unblended" from the angry part. It no longer had full control of the steering wheel. I could still feel it, yes—but now I was observing it. Witnessing it. As my "authentic self" took charge, I realized I wasn't ashamed or afraid of my anger anymore. I welcomed it. It was there to protect me.

My friend asked me to visualize my angry part. "Does it have a name? A form?"

I paused and closed my eyes. What came to me was Kali—the fierce, blue-skinned goddess with wild hair and six arms. She destroys illusion, severs what no longer serves, and clears the way for transformation and truth.

She was righteous, protective, and sacred.

My inner Kali had *awakened.*

She was not going to let me get trampled on anymore. She said I had learned my lesson, and now it was her turn. She would hold the line. She would use her knives to protect me.

I was shocked by the gratitude I felt toward her. I had always been afraid of my anger before—but this time, it didn't feel dangerous or out of control. It felt necessary. Fierce. Pure. I welcomed it.

Ryan, to his credit, had been giving me space. I was grateful for that, too. He probably thought I just needed a few days and then we'd go back to being friendly. But no. Kali had other plans for me.

With her watchful eye protecting my boundaries, I sent him a text. "Don't contact me unless it's about Quinn. Logistic only. When you pick him up, stay in your car." My therapist would have been proud of me. His advice no longer seemed extreme or unnecessary. *Fuck being amicable.*

A few days later, Ryan texted something unrelated. I didn't even read the whole thing. I just deleted it—for both of us.

A few minutes later, he replied, "Sorry. Won't do that again." And he didn't.

Holding that boundary didn't just feel powerful. It felt sacred. And with Kali by my side, I was finally—*finally*—ready to begin the slow, messy process of healing.

The first layer of the onion had peeled off.

Chapter 14. Bury Them and I'm Done

I wanted to make absolutely sure I didn't backslide again. I'd sworn I was done with Ryan before—and relapsed. Not this time.

So, first, I framed a picture of Kali and put it just inside my bedroom door. I wanted to remind myself multiple times a day that my inner Kali was here to protect me, and I needed to listen to "her" wisdom. I would stand there, looking at the image, and thank her—that part of myself. *Thank you, thank you, thank you for protecting my boundaries.* It was my new mantra, practically a prayer.

I made sure Quinn was ready to leave the house before Ryan arrived to pick him up so he could head outside as soon as his dad arrived. He caught on pretty fast and commented after a few times: "So, still don't wanna talk to Dad, huh?" he asked. "Don't blame ya."

I snorted, but repressed it quickly. *How should a mom respectfully respond to that?* "Yeah, I just need a little time away from him for now." And then I changed the subject. Quinn didn't need to carry my anger.

It was gratifying to hear he agreed that not talking to Ryan was a good idea for me, though. I tried to keep our shit away from Quinn, but of course he had noticed what was going on between his parents.

Keeping it together for Quinn was one thing. Figuring out how to let go was another.

Other than burying my feelings and hoping they'd go away, as I had done with Sebastian, I didn't know how to actually let go or how to move on. And just burying my feelings hadn't worked very well—it took me nearly fifteen years to let go of Sebastian, and I wasn't willing to let it take anywhere near that long this time.

My therapist's advice about reducing my contact with Ryan down to almost nothing had really helped when I finally followed it, so I scheduled another session with him, hoping he would have another nugget of wisdom for me.

* * *

"I want to move on. But… I really don't know how. I don't know what to do."

My therapist nodded and encouraged me to continue.

"I don't want him back. But I still feel… I don't know. Lost? Untethered? Like I'm just floating in space, waiting for something to happen. And part of me still feels like I won't really be okay until I have someone new in my life to take his place." I grimaced at myself.

He leaned forward slightly. "You've spent so much time attaching your sense of self to a relationship. It makes sense that you don't know who you are outside of that."

I narrowed my eyes at him. "I don't think that's true." Or maybe I just didn't want to believe it.

He continued as if I hadn't said anything. "It's a very common and fixable problem."

I rubbed my temples. He was giving me a headache. *A fixable* problem? I mean, who *wasn't* a little relationship-oriented? It seemed like everyone wanted to be in a relationship, and why not? When they're good, life is better. Besides, wanting to be in a relationship didn't mean I didn't know who I was. I had a career, a child, friends, hobbies. I knew who I was. Didn't I?

Maybe so, maybe not, but the truth was, I felt hollow inside. I felt incomplete now that I was single again. Maybe I was a little too focused on relationships. And maybe he had a solution.

"Okay. What should I do?"

He smiled as if he'd been waiting for that question. "Take six months for yourself."

I must have misheard. "What?" *If I had heard correctly, that's the stupidest advice ever.*

"No dating," he said. "No searching for a relationship. No swiping on apps, no 'just seeing what's out there.' Nothing."

I let out a small, incredulous laugh. "And do what? Just… stare at a wall for six months?"

He smirked. "No. You do whatever you want. Take an art class. A dance class—"

I snorted. "I *teach* dance classes."

He gave me a knowing look. "Then take a class for *yourself*. Try something new. Go to the beach with your best friend. Travel, even if it's just for a weekend. Do the things that make you feel alive again—things that have nothing to do with being someone's partner."

I rolled my eyes internally. This had *Eat Pray Love* vibes all over the place. I wanted to argue. I wanted to tell my therapist this was a waste of time, that I already knew who I was, and that I didn't need some stupid "self-discovery" period.

But I had to admit—I didn't have a better idea.

What did I have to lose? Nothing, really. I hadn't taken a break after Sebastian and I parted ways, and now I could see that jumping right back into dating had been… suboptimal. I had longed for him for years. I had taken my unhealed heart into every relationship afterwards, including well into my marriage with Ryan.

"Okay, fine, I'll try it. But if I end up a weird hermit with seven cats, painting along with Bob Ross in my living room, I'm blaming you."

He chuckled. "That's a very specific fear, but if you do, you can always come back for more advice."

* * *

As I was leaving my neighborhood to go shopping a few days later, there was a trembling lump of fur in the middle of the road. It was shaking so hard I could see it from the car. I wasn't sure what it was at first, but I pulled over to investigate. Whatever it was, I didn't want it to get run over.

It was a teeny, tiny kitten, and it was bleeding from its lip and paw. Poor little thing. There was no way I would abandon it. Instead, I abandoned my plans and took it home.

But it would be the last one. No more cats. I now had three—still technically below the threshold for being a crazy cat lady, but only just.

* * *

I took my therapist's advice to heart. As I began my six-month obligatory "me time," healing became my new hobby. I tackled it with gusto, determined to heal, find myself, and rediscover my passions—preferably within the six-month deadline. I told myself I'd be fresh and ready to dive back into the dating pool. That's how it works, right?

So, I signed up for a painting class with a few friends, which was not the same as painting alone to Bob Ross videos and absolutely did not count as becoming a hermit. I went on a weekend getaway with another friend. I journaled. I started teaching Quinn to dance because I wanted him to help me demonstrate moves in my dance classes.

I also wanted to better understand what had happened to me during my marriage and divorce. I wanted to learn from my experiences and not make the same mistakes again. So, I started reading tons of self-help books.

The one that helped the most was on adult attachment theory. I'd heard of attachment theory before—mostly regarding babies and their caregivers—but I had never thought to apply it to myself as a partner, let alone as a wife. But as I read, a light bulb turned on.

I wasn't crazy. I wasn't pathetic.

I was *normal*. My behavior was *predictable*.

According to the theory, I'd started our relationship with a secure attachment style. I was open-hearted and emotionally available. I expected connection, mutual support, and responsiveness, because that's what I had experienced in my relationship with Sebastian, even after things ended between us.

As Ryan had disappeared into his video games, causing me to feel ignored, I had slowly withdrawn. Eventually, I convinced myself I didn't care. It was easier than allowing myself to feel the pain of feeling so alone.

The shift I underwent was a classic move toward avoidant attachment in response to an emotionally unavailable partner. I wasn't cold or distant by nature, but I was subconsciously protecting myself.

When Ryan told me about his affair and was about to leave, something inside me flipped—hard.

Suddenly, I wasn't avoidant anymore.

I switched to having anxious attachment, just as the book said commonly happens after betrayal.

I clung. I begged. I pleaded. I couldn't let go, even after the divorce. Brain chemicals were literally preventing me from doing so—panic overriding reason. I was in the throes of anxious attachment gone amuck.

It was all so textbook it was almost laughable.

And yet, while living through it, I had felt like I was losing my mind. Even when I knew I was being crazy and irrational, I couldn't stop myself.

Attachment theory helped me understand Ryan, too—not in a way that excused what he did, but in a way that explained why being with him had always felt so destabilizing.

He would move toward me just enough to give me hope, and then pull away again. Every time he did, my nervous system lit up—confused, on edge, trying to reestablish connection. Even after he moved out, he kept doing it: coming close, opening up, flirting, talking about us—then disappearing again.

No wonder I couldn't let go. I wasn't responding to reality—I was responding to the intermittent closeness, the almosts, the maybes. That push–pull kept my attachment system activated and exhausted, long after the relationship itself was already over.

Reading about attachment theory didn't change what had happened. It didn't erase the humiliation of how desperately I had tried to win him back. But it gave me one thing I hadn't had before: understanding.

I finally understood that I wasn't a pathetic idiot like I had thought for most of that time. I had simply been trapped by an attachment system gone awry.

Understanding it gave me more compassion for myself and for Ryan. We were just two people in pain who didn't know how to create and maintain a healthy connection.

With this new understanding, another layer of the onion peeled off.

* * *

Understanding my attachment patterns was enlightening, but I still felt like there were deeper layers to uncover. That's when my parts work friend suggested taking my healing to the next level.

She recommended a professional IFS (Internal Family Systems) coach. IFS is the original version of parts work, and she thought I would benefit from working with a professional. My calls with her had been useful, but neither of us were IFS experts—we were more like the blind leading the blind.

I agreed a session with a professional could be useful, so I scheduled an appointment.

In my session, the IFS coach walked me through a releasing ceremony. He guided me through a conversation with Ryan's Higher Self. You know—the kind of guided inner dialogue that would've sounded ridiculous to me once, and now felt completely natural.

"Tell Ryan's Higher Self everything you appreciated about him, what you blamed him for, and what you projected onto him."

I closed my eyes and imagined him sitting in front of me. "Ryan, I appreciated you believing me about the spiritual message and taking the leap with me to have Quinn. I blamed you for neglecting me—for choosing escape over our marriage. I projected my fear of abandonment onto you."

"Good, now admit your faults."

"Ryan, I expected you to fulfill my needs without clearly telling you what they were. I expected you to be someone you weren't."

It was healing to admit my role in our decline. I wasn't just a helpless victim at the whims of the world. Victims have no control over anything; they can't make changes for the better. I wanted to take full control of my life.

"What did Ryan appreciate about you, and what did he blame you for?"

I had to think for a moment. I hadn't felt appreciated in a long time, but I finally came up with something. "He appreciated my positive energy. He blamed me for not being supportive enough, for not unconditionally supporting him." How could I when I had thought Ryan made one bad decision after another? We had been so mismatched from the beginning, and it was good to be reminded of that.

"Very good," he reassured me. "Now, imagine a cord, a fuzzy white light, connecting your hearts. Use the cord to take back everything of yours from Ryan and give everything of his back to him."

This was so much like the cord-cutting ceremony I had done on my own with Sebastian ten years earlier. I really hoped I wouldn't pop my shoulders out of their sockets this time.

I refocused and visualized an energy exchange, and I could practically feel the baggage between us disappearing.

"Now, gently sever the cord and wrap the loose ends in healing light. Send Ryan's half back to him and bring your half into your heart."

This was a much gentler approach than I had taken with Sebastian, but as I mentally severed the cord, a wave of unexpected emotion surged through me. I suddenly started crying and couldn't stop.

"What's going on?" he asked gently.

"It's hard to let go… Part of me doesn't want to. I don't know why. I really thought I was ready…"

He had me focus on the part that didn't want to let go. I realized it was very young, maybe four or five years old. She was trying to hide, and she thought I needed a man for protection. Ryan had been that part's protector for so long, and she didn't want to let go.

She didn't need Ryan—she just believed I needed someone, anyone, to protect me.

Letting go was too scary for this vulnerable part of me—I didn't have someone else lined up to take his place.

"Let's do a life review with that part," the IFS coach said. "Show her you're all grown up now and don't need a protector anymore."

I visualized my life—my kindergarten to PhD education, my two marriages, and having a child of my own. I also showed my younger self the strength I had developed over the years.

"What does this part need?" he asked.

I checked in with her. She wanted protection—certainty that someone strong was standing guard.

Instead of searching for something new, I felt Kali step forward—fierce, uncompromising. She knelt beside the child part, not to soothe, but to stand between her and anything that would harm her. Watching. Choosing. Deciding what would remain.

The message was clear: *Nothing gets to you without going through me.*

The child part's grip loosened. She finally understood.

I was never unprotected.

As the session ended, I felt wrung out, but in a good way.

I hadn't known how deeply part of me believed I needed a protector.

No wonder I'd clung so hard.

Letting go had felt like danger.

And with that, another layer of the onion peeled off.

* * *

After that session, I noticed something strange. I had stopped scanning every room for potential partners.

It was the oddest thing. I just stopped wanting to date.

For the first time in my life, I didn't feel like I needed a man—and that felt almost unbelievable. Maybe someday I'd want one again. But the needing part was over.

My six months of me-time ended with me not changing anything at all. I had expected to reenter the dating pool once the clock ran out, but I didn't. I just kept living.

I also stopped believing healing had to be finished on a schedule.

I might have just kept journaling, reading, and going to therapy. But then I heard about a week-long healing retreat in Maui, and I just knew I had to go.

For years, the noise of my life had drowned out that inner pull. Now things were quiet enough to hear it again. So I listened. And I went.

* * *

The first few days of the retreat were full of practices that started cracking my heart wide open.

In the ho'oponopono ceremony, I whispered words I wasn't sure I meant yet—*I'm sorry. Please forgive me. Thank you. I love you.* Saying them aloud softened something inside me anyway.

The "core emotions dance" helped me embrace feelings I'd spent years avoiding—and left me ecstatic. During the ocean cleansing, it felt like the salt water pulled… something… out of me that didn't belong there. Daily yoga loosened emotional blockages I hadn't even known were still lodged in my body.

It wasn't one dramatic breakthrough. It was more like a steady unlocking.

I felt stronger. Lighter. Closer to being fully healed—but not quite there yet.

Additional healers were available for private sessions, so I signed up to work with Vee, a renowned energy and spiritual healer. I'd heard about her remarkable abilities—but also that no two sessions were ever the same. Whatever happened, I'd have to experience it for myself.

I didn't know what to expect. But I knew I was ready.

* * *

The moment I entered Vee's healing space, she opened her eyes and looked slightly surprised to see me.

"Ahhh," she said with a small smile, "so you decided to come in person."

I paused in the doorway. "Have we talked before?" I was pretty sure this was our first contact of any kind, other than me signing my name on the session sheet.

"Not physically," she said. "But your spirit visited me last night."

I considered myself spiritually open-minded, but this was a stretch, even for me.

"It came to check on me," she continued. "To see if this was the right place for you, if your heart would be safe with me." She rested a hand over her own chest. "It wanted reassurance that I could help you break what still binds you."

A warm shiver swept through my whole body. I didn't know how spirits made appointments, but apparently mine had shown up early.

Something in me relaxed.

"Well," she said, gesturing for me to sit, "your spirit was very clear. You're ready. Tell me about your ex—that's the crux of the issue, right?"

My breath caught. Something in me recognized it—a quiet yes, like I'd already been there.

I sat down and started telling her my story.

"I don't want Ryan back," I finished, "but I feel like there's still… something there. Like I'm still connected to him somehow, and I don't know how to break the connection."

Vee nodded and closed her eyes. I assumed she was seeking the connection.

"You've already weakened the bonds to Ryan," she said softly. "But there's still some energetic residue in your womb from him."

A chill ran through me.

I knew *exactly* what she meant. And it creeped me out.

No matter how much physical or emotional distance I'd put between us, something still lingered—and I wanted it *gone*.

With my permission to remove the bond, Vee began moving her hands gracefully through the air as she chanted softly and shook rattles. I closed my eyes and focused on my breath. I tried to stay relaxed, but I could feel the tension in me. This just *had* to work. I desperately wanted to be free from him in every way.

She worked her way from my head to my womb. After a bit of rattle shaking above my womb, she suddenly grabbed at my womb repeatedly and tugged at something that connected deep inside.

Then… it just gave way.

The final time she tugged, it felt like something energetically gripping at my womb let go and was just… gone.

"There," Vee said, holding up a small pebble. "I placed the bond in here. When you leave, bury it outside my door, in the heart of Maui. That way, neither of you has to carry this connection anymore."

I stared at the tiny stone. My fingers tingled as I took it from her. Could this really be it? The final release?

"Ryan was destined to father your child," Vee continued when I looked up. "But he was never meant to be your forever partner. Your soul contract with him was complete by the time Quinn was one," she said—and something in me recognized it instantly. "You went above and beyond—giving him more time as a family, giving him more time with Quinn."

Her words hit like a revelation—and I suddenly knew it was true.

The years of struggle. The effort to hold our family together. The mistaken belief that leaving him would mean I was a failure.

It all made sense now.

My karma with Ryan had long since been complete. I had done my part. I could let our relationship go. I could *finally* let go of it completely.

Then Vee's expression shifted slightly.

"But I felt another bond—a weak one connected to your heart chakra. It wasn't Ryan. Who would that be?"

My breath caught.

Of course.

"Sebastian. My first husband. I thought that bond was gone."

It had been over five years since we'd spoken. I hadn't felt the familiar deep longing for him during our last conversation or afterward, so I assumed the tie had finally faded.

Vee shook her head gently. "Your heart still holds a faint connection to him. Even with minimal contact, the bond hasn't fully closed. He must have been the one who opened your heart the most."

I had never thought of it that way, but he was. He had been my deepest love.

Now it was time to let him go completely, too.

Again, with my permission to remove this bond, Vee chanted and shook her rattles. This time, the release was very gentle, like having your hand let go from a gentle handhold. Even so, letting go stirred more emotion than I expected.

I hadn't realized how much of me had still been holding space for him in the quiet corners of my heart.

I had unknowingly remained tethered to both of my ex-husbands, and now suddenly, I wasn't.

It felt like I had been wearing ankle and wrist weights, and they had been removed. For the first time in twenty years, I could finally move freely.

I buried both pebbles in the volcanic soil beneath a plumeria tree outside Vee's cabin. I pressed my palms into the warm earth and thanked the land for holding what I no longer needed to carry. Then I thanked them both—and let them go.

I walked away from the cabin, brushing the dirt from my palms. I realized I wasn't carrying anything anymore—not hope, not longing, not vigilance.

This wasn't relief.

It was surrender.

And for the first time, surrender didn't feel like giving up. It felt like making space for whatever came next.

* * *

The activity the next morning was a meditation walk in the Maui forest. Our guide told us to stick to the main path—unless we felt a strong pull to leave it. The idea was to let the forest speak to us, to guide us where we needed to go.

I didn't think I had anything left to heal after my private session with Vee, so I assumed I would just have a nice stroll along the main path.

After about ten minutes, though, I felt compelled to leave the path. I felt a flicker of annoyance. I just wanted to have a relaxing walk, but the tug was clear, so I climbed over a small ridge. There, nestled among the trees, hidden from the main trail, sticks and flowers were carefully arranged into a six-foot wide heart with a peace sign in the middle.

I was stunned. It didn't feel like a coincidence. I'd been led here.

I just stared at it for a few moments. Then I stepped into the heart and sat down, being careful not to move any of the sticks or flowers.

As I sat there and breathed in the quiet, sacred energy of the forest, strange thoughts began swirling in my mind.

What if everything had been exactly as it needed to be? What if Sebastian had been nearly perfect, precisely because he couldn't stay?

And what if Ryan's affair—devastating as it was—had been the exact catalyst I needed to stop seeking validation outside myself?

They were wild ideas, almost too big to consider. But sitting in that heart-shaped space, they felt true. Maybe it had all unfolded exactly as it needed to.

Sebastian had taught me what deep love felt like. Ryan had taught me what my own strength looked like.

Maybe we'd all been exactly who we needed to be for each other, even when it hurt… especially when it hurt.

I felt a surprising wave of gratitude for Ryan's affair. It didn't create the cracks. It revealed them. The betrayal hurt—but what shattered me was realizing how much of the story I'd written myself.

Without the affair, we might have stayed together indefinitely—functional on the surface, but quietly unhappy underneath. We'd been holding each other hostage. Now we were free.

I had resisted letting go, convinced we were supposed to stay together *no matter what.* I clung so tightly to the dream of what I thought we were meant to be that I nearly missed who we actually were.

I didn't think I'd misheard the spirit—I'd misunderstood the duration of the soul contract. We'd been meant to bring Quinn into the world together, but after that, our paths had been free to diverge.

Now that we were no longer trying to force a marriage to work, we could be amicable co-parents without making each other miserable.

It had taken so long to let go of Sebastian because, deep down, I hadn't wanted to. I'd missed how he made me feel. I'd kept hoping our love would rewrite reality. Learning the difference between love and fantasy had been one of my hardest lessons.

And yet—both relationships had brought me here. Both had taught me what love is and what it isn't.

Maybe that was part of the journey too—learning when to hold on, when to let go, and how to gather the wisdom that comes after the fire.

As I sat there in the forest's heart, I no longer felt like *Minnie*, the version of me who had settled, who had kept herself small to fit in. I had outgrown her.

I had become *Minerva*.

Not the goddess—just a woman who'd earned her wisdom the hard way.

I'd spent years waiting to be completed by someone else.

No one was coming.

Nothing was missing.

Like that heart in the forest, I was whole.

Epilogue

It's been a year and a half since the Maui retreat, and three years since Disclosure Day. When Ryan confessed his affair that holiday morning, I didn't know July 4th would become my Personal Independence Day—but it has.

And here I am this year—on a dance floor, leading. Not just dancing—leading. Just like in the rest of my life now.

I'm out with my new friend, Grace. We found each other through ballroom dancing, bonding over a shared love of dance—and our respective divorces—and I couldn't be happier.

As we waltz around the dance floor, I can't help but think about how much has changed since I decided to lead in life, not just in dance. This isn't the life I once planned, but it has its perks. Let's be real—I don't have a husband, but I *do* have a vibrator. It doesn't run to the store when I'm out of avocados, but it doesn't hog the covers or snore either. Worth it.

I also have my red velvet couch. I spend a lot of time on it—reading, resting, and generally treating it like the throne it is. When my sister first saw it, she later told me she'd thought, *of course—that's her.* She hadn't known all the details of my marriage, but she'd watched me fade. The bold red told her I was back, long before I realized it myself.

But I wasn't just back—I was different. The woman who'd owned pink shag rugs had been bold, yes, but she'd been rebuilding from a marriage that left her questioning her own desirability. She'd reclaimed her confidence in every way but one—she was still desperate for a man to prove she was worth wanting. The red couch woman is not.

The couch itself—sensual, decadent, built for pleasure—sits proudly in my bedroom next to my single bed. Designed for my comfort alone.

I know what it feels like to be truly seen and deeply loved—and I've learned that wanting that isn't asking too much. That was Sebastian's lasting gift.

If I ever settle down again, it'll be because some man capable of a deep, mutually satisfying connection made me want to share my couch—and because we enhance each other. Not because I'm afraid to be alone. Oh, and he'll be an amazing ballroom dancer. Not asking for much, am I?

Still, I'm open to it, but I'm not looking for it. I'm too damn busy loving my life. Turns out, rock bottom is one hell of a trampoline.

The biggest surprise?

I love being a single mom.

I'd fought it since Quinn was in utero—turns out, it's one of the greatest joys of my life.

One of the best parts is that Quinn, now almost fifteen, helps me teach my dance classes. I don't actually need an assistant, but I love having him beside me, demonstrating moves and charming the ladies. He's taken a special liking to swing dancing, and it fills my heart to watch his confidence blossom. If I were still with Ryan, that never would've happened.

Split custody? That fear turned out to be unfounded, too. Honestly, I enjoy the quiet me time when he's with his dad—and hey, I can even walk around naked and talk to my plants like they're dear friends. What's not to like?

In fact, Quinn is off spending a month with his dad—and Roxanne. Shockingly, she finally moved in with Ryan, and they moved to another state over a year ago. Good thing I never actually bet my house and legs—I still need them. I'm truly happy for the little love birds, though… especially now that I don't have to worry about running into them anywhere. Just because I'm happy for them doesn't mean I want to *see* them.

As we waltz around the dance floor again, I lead Grace through a pattern she doesn't know, and she grins at me mid-way through it. "You're the best lead here, Minerva. Seriously. I'd follow you anywhere."

I laugh. "Well, I finally cracked the code."

"Oh, and what's the code?"

"You have to trust yourself first."

"Oh my gosh." Grace shakes her head. "Only you could turn a waltz into a life lesson."

"Took me over twenty years and two divorces to figure that out. You're welcome."

"Well, I'd still follow you anywhere."

"Careful—I've married for less."

We both burst out laughing, and I lead her into a dramatic spin as the music carries us forward.

Reflections for Your Own Journey

You've now seen what it looks like when I ignore my instincts, override reality, and convince myself something is meant to be.

You may have recognized parts of yourself in that. Or not. Either way, this isn't about me anymore.

The questions below are here to help you look at your own patterns and how these themes show up in your life. As you move through them, notice not just your reactions to my story, but what it reflects back to you.

You don't need to answer all of them. Just start with the ones that feel a little too relevant to ignore.

Self-Awareness & Patterns

1. What recurring patterns have shown up in your relationships or major life decisions?
2. When have you ignored something you knew, deep down, to be true?
3. How have your past experiences shaped the expectations you carry into new situations?

Relationships & Emotional Needs

1. What does a fulfilling relationship look like to you—and where did that definition come from?
2. How do you typically respond when your emotional needs are not met?
3. Have you ever stayed in a relationship longer than you knew you should? What made it difficult to leave?
4. In what ways do you give and receive love, and how well are those needs communicated?

Identity & Personal Growth

1. In what ways have you changed yourself to maintain a relationship or meet someone else's expectations?
2. When have you felt most like your authentic self?
3. What parts of yourself have you minimized, hidden, or abandoned over time?
4. What would it look like to fully reclaim those parts of yourself?

Intuition, Belief & Meaning

1. How do you distinguish between intuition and wishful thinking?
2. What role do your beliefs—spiritual or otherwise—play in your decision-making?
3. When has your inner voice guided you well, and has it ever led you in a direction you later questioned?

Boundaries & Decision-Making

1. What boundaries are easiest for you to maintain? Which are the most difficult?
2. How do you typically respond when someone crosses your boundaries?
3. What would it look like to make decisions from a place of clarity rather than urgency?

Desire, Worth & Fulfillment

1. What do you believe you need in order to feel complete or fulfilled?
2. Where have you looked outside yourself for validation or a sense of worth?
3. What does a deeply satisfying and aligned life look like for you now?

Take what resonates. Leave the rest.
And maybe trust yourself first this time.

Book Club Discussion Questions

This story tends to provoke opinions.

Some choices may seem obvious in hindsight. Others may feel more complicated the longer you sit with them.

These questions are meant to open up conversation about what you noticed, what you questioned, and how you made sense of it.

You don't have to agree—honestly, it's more interesting if you don't.

Character & Perspective

1. How did your perception of the narrator evolve over the course of the book?
2. In what ways did you relate to her experiences or internal conflicts?
3. Were there moments when you felt frustrated with her choices? Why?
4. How did her self-awareness (or lack of it at times) shape your reading experience?

Relationships & Dynamics

1. What patterns do you notice in the narrator's relationships?
2. What early signs or red flags were present, and how were they interpreted or overlooked?
3. How did differences in communication styles and emotional needs impact the relationship?
4. To what extent do you think compatibility versus effort determines the success of a relationship?

Decision-Making & Turning Points

1. Which decisions in the book felt most pivotal or consequential?
2. How did urgency influence the narrator's choices throughout the story?

3. Were there moments where a different choice might have significantly altered the outcome?
4. How do you interpret the balance between intention, timing, and circumstance in her decisions?

Belief, Intuition & Interpretation

1. How did you interpret the spiritual experiences described in the book?
2. In what ways did belief—whether intuitive, emotional, or spiritual—shape the narrator's actions?
3. Do you see these moments as guidance, projection, or something else entirely?
4. How might different readers interpret these experiences differently?

Themes & Takeaways

1. What do you see as the central themes of the memoir?
2. What do you think the narrator ultimately learned about herself?
3. How does the concept of personal responsibility show up throughout the story?
4. What message, if any, did you take away about love, identity, or growth?

Reflection & Connection

1. Which moments or themes felt most relevant to your own life or observations?
2. Did the story challenge or reinforce any of your existing beliefs about relationships?
3. What conversations did this book spark for you?
4. How might this story influence the way you think about your own decisions or patterns?

If nothing else, consider this a cautionary tale—
now you know what not to do.

Acknowledgments

I want to thank:

All the people in my life who appear in this story. When lived experience becomes memoir, real people inevitably become characters—not fictionalized, but remembered, interpreted, and rendered through a single point of view. This book reflects my experience of those relationships, not an objective accounting of who anyone "really" is. Thank you for being part of the moments that shaped both my life and this story.

Matt Rudd and his *Punchy Books Accelerator* course, which I found while looking for a new, post-divorce hobby. It ultimately led me to decide that writing a memoir would be a good idea.

Wendy Dale and her *Memoir Writing for Geniuses* course, along with my coach, **Tanya Whitehead**. They taught me how to write a memoir—specifically, how to turn a rambling, unstructured mess into something resembling actual chapters with actual scenes.

My writing group—Julie Marr, Andrea Lawrence, Jim Pollock, and Maureen Migrditchian—for reading the messy early drafts, asking hard questions, and helping make this book far better than it would have been otherwise.

About the Author

Minerva Morehart holds a PhD in psychology, which she eventually turned inward while navigating divorce, healing, and a long-overdue reckoning with herself. She writes at the intersection of professional insight and lived experience, exploring psychology, spirituality, and the work of becoming whole after collapse.

She lives in Ohio with her son, dog, and three cats, where she dances and continues building a life that fits.

You can find her at **minervamorehart.com**, where the conversation continues—with more reflections, more uncomfortable questions, and hopefully fewer catastrophic learning experiences (no promises).

The boundaries remain firm—and the red velvet couch is still absolutely non-negotiable.

Help a Minerva

If this story moved you, unsettled you, annoyed you, or cracked something open, I'd be deeply grateful if you'd leave a review on Amazon or Goodreads.

Not a polite review.
Not a "five stars because she seems nice" review.
An *honest* one.

Tell other humans what this book actually *did* to you.
Even a sentence helps.

Did it make you laugh at wildly inappropriate moments?
Make you rethink your last three relationships?
Make you whisper "oh no" to yourself at 2 a.m.?

Say that.

Reviews help this book find the readers who need it most.

And thank you for bearing witness to this *"spiritual awakening disguised as a relationship disaster"*—which, frankly, is a growth strategy I don't recommend, even if it works.

With love and excellent boundaries,

Minerva

www.ingramcontent.com/pod-product-compliance
Lightning Source LLC
LaVergne TN
LVHW090512110826
845146LV00003B/832